# NIGHT
## OF
# MIST

## EUGENE HEIMLER

### Introduction by Eli Wiesel

*To Lily*
*without whom I would not have*
*found life again*

# Other Books by Eugene Heimler

*A LINK IN THE CHAIN*

*RESISTANCE AGAINST TYRANNY*

*MENTAL ILLNESS AND SOCIAL WORK*

*SURVIVAL IN SOCIETY*

*THE STORM*

*THE HEALING ECHO*

*MESSAGES: A SURVIVOR's LETTER TO A YOUNG GERMAN*

*MY LIFE AFTER AUSCHWITZ (ALSO UNDER THE TITLE A LINK IN THE CHAIN)*

*CONSTRUCTIVE USE OF DESTRUCTIVE FORCES (ALSO UNDER THE TITLE SURVIVAL IN SOCIETY)*

**For more information contact:**

*mheimler1@gmail.com*

*The hand of the Lord was upon me, and carried me out in the spirit of the Lord, and set me down in the midst of the valley which was full of bones,*

*And caused me to pass by them round about: and, behold, there were very many in the open valley, and, lo, they were very dry.*

*And He said unto me, Son of man, can these bones live? And I answered: O Lord God, Thou knowest.*

*— Ezekiel XXXVI: 1–4*

# Praise for *Night of the Mist*

A dramatic and readable book.

*The Times Literary Supplement*

Behind the eerie, the manic, the disgusting, he still conveys the desirability of life, the variety of human behavior, the power of imagination. His own conclusions were not of hate, but of discriminating tolerance.

**Peter Vansittart in *The Observer* (London, England)**

This book deserves a place of its own in the literature of Nazi horrors, as it deals with those events from an unusual aspect – the effect of them upon the victims themselves.

**Lord Russell of Liverpool**

There is no self-pity in Heimler's writing; just wonder at man's inhumanity to man ... the message he brings is not one of horror but of hope; of a fight back to life, and a life well worth living.

*The Huddersfield Examiner*

This book has an important lesson to teach – that faith in God and in the dignity of man can overcome the greater evils that men can devise."

*The Catholic Times*

# FOREWORD

Eugene Heimler was blessed with the love of three extraordinary women. There was his teenage sweetheart Eva whom he married in the shadow of the Nazi guns and whom he lost a few days later to the unutterable horrors of the Shoah. There was Lily, his second wife, who nurtured him back to health and hope, who gave him his children as well as his will to live... and who died of cancer after a long and brave struggle. And then there is Miriam, his student, then colleague, then wife, whose fierce loyalty and love made his last few years serene and happy.

We owe a deep debt of gratitude to Miriam Bracha Heimler for, at long last, making *Night of the Mist* – already a recognized classic in Britain, Europe and America – available in Israel too. Eugene Heimler, like his own late father, was a life-long Zionist, one who did his utmost to support the birth, and then success, of the Jewish State. While his work anchored him to the English-speaking countries on both sides of the Atlantic Ocean, he continued to the end to cherish the hope of eventually settling in Israel. Had he not died tragically early in 1990, he would surely have fulfilled his vision of living out his years in a small house in the Galilee, with a glimpse of the shore of Lake Kinneret. Providence decreed otherwise, alas. But his literary and spiritual legacy clearly belongs to his Jewish people – and their miraculously reborn state – more than to any other part of humankind.

Over half a century has passed since the events described in *Night of the Mist*.

It has been two decades since his own death in London on a cold, grey winter's day. But the story he tells is vividly, immortally alive. It is a tale of horror and heartbreak, of loss and degradation – yet also of hope and faith and warmth and humor and immortal humanity. It is unlike any other work that came out of the ashes of World War Two. His is a poet's voice as well as a philosopher's and a psychologist's. It is a young voice, an ageless voice. Our lives are the fuller for listening to it.

Rabbi Dr. André Ungar

# ACKNOWLEDGEMENTS

I wish to express my deepest thanks to Dr. André Ungar, the translator of this book, to Mrs. Rosemary Russell, who helped me to organize the material and to Miss Ruth Gordon, who offered her valuable time to type the manuscript.

– Eugene Heimler

# Introduction

## *Elie Wiesel*

Published in London almost forty years ago, Eugene Heimler's book is now, thank God, being reprinted. This will ensure its rightful place in the literature of the Holocaust. I read it at the time, and have just reread it. It is a human document of great value. It contains wounds, both familiar and less familiar, that will long haunt the reader.

I met the author in London but we could have met earlier in one of the weird crossroads of the kingdom of Night. A psychiatrist, he devoted himself to healing the mutilated souls of life's victims. He who had known the unfathomable and infinite power of evil tried to ease the burdens of suffering. I remember his voice. And his eyes.

Eugene was 21 when he arrived at Birkenau. His description of what he saw, heard and lived through is sincere and restrained. He tells wonderful and moving stories of his childhood and adolescence in Hungary – his first loves and youthful reveries – the sudden German occupation – the wedding in the ghetto. The beginnings of fear, the intimations of the trials to come. The rebellion against destiny: Eugene and his loved one are married, but their happiness lasts only one night. Their honeymoon is spent in a sealed boxcar heading towards the unknown.

This gripping account is profoundly honest. The astounding episodes he relates are both atrocious and bizarre. In Auschwitz, a few paces from the crematoriums, the daughter of the chief of a Gypsy camp takes a liking to him. She feeds and protects him. They make love. In Auschwitz. Later on, a *Lageraltester* (head of the camp) takes notice of him. Thanks to an SS officer, he is put in charge of a group of ten young prisoners. Surely a guardian angel is watching over him. On the edge of despair, a man consoles him; it is the rabbi who officiated at his marriage so many eternities ago.

These miraculous moments were more often than not engulfed in the all-encompassing climate of brutality. Heimler captures it well. The stark dehumanization of some, the desperate solidarity of others. The pangs of hunger; the power of attraction of a piece of bread. The disappearance of all traces of civilization, culture, morality. The conversations about the past, meditations on God, the dreams that make waking harder, more unbearable. How did Heimler manage to survive death, the ugly death that never ceased to stalk him? The selections, the blows, the nights of despair. It would have been so easy, so tempting to let oneself fall into the gaping abyss. In those sorrowful times for mankind, it was easier to die than live.

How can we explain the tenacity, the will to resist, to last out the death camps? Some survivors talk about the will to survive – which is something different – in order to bear witness in the name of History. Was this enough to slip through the net? How can we grasp the faith that this implies, the faith in man, if not in God? How can we believe in the future or in eternity in a place where the future of men was flouted and annihilated?

We have no answers to any of these questions. But to face them better, we must read testimonies by these witnesses, spared by a whim of fate to give memory a chance to vanquish death.

(Translated from the French by Esther Singer)

*By the end of 1941 Hitler had already come to the conclusion that the measures taken to punish those who committed offences against the German occupation were inadequate. He decided, therefore, that in future the only cases to be brought to trial before the German military courts would be those which could be presented within eight days of the commission of the offence and in which a sentence of death was certain to be awarded. Accordingly, he issued the "Nacht und Nebel" (Night and Fog) decree of December 7, 1941. Its object was to ensure that non-German civilians in occupied territories, alleged to have committed offences against the occupation forces, were taken secretly to Germany, hence its name, unless it could be guaranteed that a death sentence would be passed if they were tried by a military court in their own country. Hitler took the view that the only way to deter potential offenders was to take such measures as would leave their families and the local population uncertain of their fate.*

# CHAPTER I

The sun scorched down on a world which was whirling round me. Black spots were dancing before my eyes and the longing for water stabbed through my body.

"Water!"

It was the only word, the only thought I could hold on to.

Down the long road leading from the station a line of people were dragging [along with] slow, weary steps. Here and there a face seemed to bear some obscure message which I could not read. Stumbling between the rails, I was reminded of the station in my own town many, many years ago, on a day of very similar coloring. I felt as if I were back at the station – that if I took the first turning on the left, I would be in King Street; left again at the first corner and I would be home.

I stepped out of the line and started walking away, as if driven by the force of memories back toward the old, familiar streets. A harsh shout stopped me. Something heavy and black struck me, and everything went dark.

Someone was calling from the bottom of the staircase:

"Martha, is the master in? Maaartha…. Maaaaaaartha…." The echoing aaa's filled the dim staircase. Slowly I opened my eyes. I was lying on the ground; blood was oozing from the corner of my mouth. I could see people's feet, the color of their trousers. Sand tasted foul on my tongue.

*"Aufstehn! Steh' auf!"* (Get up! Up!) Somebody pulled me up. A man in uniform stood before me.

"How old are you?"

"Twenty-two," I whispered as if in a trance.

1

*"Gesund?"* (Healthy?)

I did not reply.

*"Gesund?"* I heard again. The voice seemed to come from a long way off.

I nodded. But I must be ill, I thought. How strange everything is here – my head is buzzing – there is pain in my lips – somebody must have struck me just now. Someone is shouting up the staircase – there's a queer smell in the air – why is that odd-looking barrack standing there instead of King Street to the left of the station? – I ought to go home.

The crowd swept me along. On both sides of the road men in pyjama jackets were breaking stones, their hammers gleaming in the sunshine. As we passed by them they whispered up to us: "Give us your spoons, knives, anything you've got. They'll take everything off you." I could not understand what they were talking about.

Skull and crossbones stared from the fences.... "Danger! High Tension."

They gave us a mug each and we drank for the first time in days. The water was the color of mud and smelled bad.

On we swayed. Iron gates opened and closed behind us. The road was now lined with trees; the rays of the sun danced feverishly [upon] their leaves. Someone spoke to me:

"See this knot?" He pointed at his handkerchief, knotted in the corner. "I tied it before they pushed us into the truck. I tied it at home. And now I don't know what it was for." He stared ahead in unseeing despair.

We reached a large glass pavilion, were ordered to strip naked. Over our heads water suddenly started to run, hot and cold, cold and hot; alternately. Some barbers came in; with electric machines they had shaved us bare within seconds.

"I can't understand, I can't understand – where am I? – at home? Yes, of course, near the swimming pool..." The screams which continually pierced my ears were only the squeals of bathers pushed playfully into the water. "Someone is waiting for me at the corner of the Grand Café – I ought to get dressed." Time rose and fell, as inexorable as a whip across one's back. Ouch....

Somebody had given me a merciless blow. Blood began to trickle from my nose, and the pain brought the past flooding back into my mind. At last I was able to retrace the steps in the line that led from home to here and now.

In the spring of 1944 Germany overran Hungary. German tanks and armored cars roared through the town by the thousand; the evening wind blew cold, Teutonic songs into our rooms through the windows, which we kept open at night, ready for escape at any moment. The Nazis did not keep us waiting long.

A few days later some plainclothes Gestapo officers arrested my father in the street in front of our house. Since the day of the invasion I had tried to persuade him to flee to Budapest, where he could have disappeared among a million others in the city. But, apart from being a Socialist, he was also a deeply religious man (the two traits can exist harmoniously side by side, whatever Karl Marx may say), and he replied that one should acquiesce in the will of God, that he was no longer young, and that he had lived most of his allotted span already.

"If the end must come, let it come," he said.

From the widow of our flat I watched helplessly as they pushed the sick, grey-haired man into a car. For a few seconds his image remained with me; then the car turned the corner. I never saw him again.

In the street people had thickened into a crowd. They knew my father, knew that all his life he had stood by the side of the oppressed. He was loved and respected for it.

The color left their faces as they watched his arrest, and afterwards they dispersed slowly, without a word. There was something in the way those people walked, in the light of the setting sun, which reminded me of a funeral. When – before the war – we had buried Mother after a long illness and I had returned to the old familiar furniture upon which her eyes had so often rested, I glanced out into the street and saw the people who had come to offer their condolences. In their slow departure, in the crimson of the sinking sun, there was the same sad rhythm that marked the disappearance of my father in the Gestapo car.

I realized that I, too, was in danger, that from now on I was no longer at home in my native land. The Germans were accustomed to arrest the whole family, not merely its head. "If they arrest me, Jancsi," my father had said, "go to Dr. Tanka, the Medical Superintendent of the Mental Hospital. I believe he is an honest man. Ask him to take you in – there you may be able to escape a similar fate."

I decided to leave our flat and go to my sweetheart, Eva. Gradually I began to say my farewells – to the garden in which I had spent the most beautiful years of my childhood; to the trees on which I had carved lovers' hearts that had stretched with the growth of the bark through the years; to the arbor where I had first kissed a girl; to the red garden chairs on which I had so often sat with father, mother and sister; to the streets in which I could have found my way blindfold.

It was an odd feeling to walk, stealthily as a murderer, along those familiar streets; to dart through the back entrances of buildings which the Germans had not yet learnt to control; to take refuge from an approaching German in a doorway where once I had played hide-and-seek with my friends.

My arrival was received by Eva's parents with mixed feelings. Eva's mother was worried lest someone had followed me, and that by giving me shelter the whole family would be endangered, while her father was glad that I had come and expressed his opinion of the Gestapo in unrepeatable terms. Through a sleepless night Eva and I tried to sort out our uncertain future, and decided that on the morrow I would go along to Dr. Tanka and that, if possible, she would join me at the hospital later.

In the morning I asked Eva to spy out the land for me at our flat, in order to find out if the police or Gestapo were still there. I waited in the park not far away, and when she signaled that all was clear I joined her. I knew then that I should never set foot amongst the familiar furniture again, that strangers, Nazis, would soon move in and take over everything that my parents had worked for throughout their life. I have never had a destructive nature, but now I decided to destroy everything in the house – furniture, carpets, pictures, clothing. With an axe I chopped the beautiful furniture to matchwood; with a knife I ripped the pictures, paintings and carpets; and I broke everything I could lay my hands on. Eva helped me in this cold-blooded but purposeful destruction. When everything was destroyed, I left the flat, taking with me a pair of shirts and some pictures of my family, and went to the Mental Hospital. The Superintendent accepted me, and I was given a room on the second floor.

This floor accommodated people suffering from minor nervous disorders. Every night through the open window I could hear occasional screams from the unfortunate ones on the ground and first floors where the more seriously afflicted patients lived. Fear kept me awake for whole nights on end, and the nightmarish atmosphere of the hospital increased my incessant anxiety for my father, my family, Eva, my friends and my country, and for my own struggle against a hopeless and confused future. On the third sleepless night, lying in a pool of perspiration with my heart beating like a drum in the jungle, I felt that I myself had reached the edge of insanity, and wanted to cry out to the cold sky and beyond the night to the sleeping lights for help. I imagined myself doomed to become just another of these demented outcasts shrieking in the night. I called to the nurse that I could not stay in my room alone any longer, and she sent up the doctor on night duty, a Polish prisoner of war who had been allowed to work at his own profession. Unkempt, and at first sleepy, he sat down by my bedside, and I told him everything that lay heavy on my heart.

He listened quietly to my story, and then he said:

"Mr. Heimler, you're not one of Nietzsche's Supermen. You are simply a youth of twenty-one. If any sane youth of twenty-one were placed in the circumstances you're in now, it would be a sign of abnormality if he were not afraid. I do not know what the future has in store for you. But what I do know is this. If ever you manage to survive all this alive and sane, you will have learnt that there are two types of persecution in the world. One comes from without: different dictatorships, under different colors, can put the noose around one's neck and, indirectly around one's soul. The other persecution comes from within, and this is the persecution from which our patients are suffering. Never believe, Mr. Heimler, that it is only you and I who are oppressed by a cruel power. Millions of free men, living in the free lands of the world, are similarly oppressed. They are persecuted by the dark forces in their own souls."

When once again I was left by myself in my room, I felt much easier in my mind. My suffering and despair were, after all, only relative matters. My own oppression might one day come to an end, but these wretched creatures below would still be slaves even when I was free.

Next day I received a visitor, Eva's father. We sat out in the large garden. On the benches around us some of the patients sat quietly talking to themselves; others paced diligently up and down the narrow, sunlit garden path as if it were a job for which they would be paid; others still stood in rigid, statuesque poses, staring into nothingness. It was a beautiful May day; the sky lavished love on the earth in abundance.

Mr. Kallus looked around the garden. He shuddered a little, in spite of the warmth.

"How can you bear it here, my boy? Even to look at it makes me shiver." He filled his pipe. "D'you know why I've come?"

"Yes. Because of Eva."

He nodded, somewhat embarrassed. Croaking, he cleared his throat and said:

"As you know, Eva loves you, and she wants to be your wife."

"I know," I replied. "I want to marry her."

He was silent for a moment, then continued:

"It would be difficult for you to come to town; besides, it would be dangerous. I can see to the formalities, then you can sneak in and get married. Under ordinary circumstances I would have advised you to wait till both of you were a little older, and until you could earn your own livelihood. But these times are not normal, and as far as a profession is concerned, who knows what the future will bring? They say," his voice faltered, "they say that the Germans won't harm German women." Tears gathered in his eyes, "I wouldn't like anything to happen to my little girl. Do you understand?"

"I understand."

"It is rumored that some Jewish girls will be taken to Germany, and..."

"I too have heard it."

Mr. Kallus sat in the middle of the perambulating circle of the demented, tears streaming from his eyes.

"What a world! That I should have to discuss the future of my daughter – here."

"It is a mad world, Mr. Kallus."

He nodded. Then we shook hands, and he started walking toward the gate.

A week later I received a letter informing me that the wedding would take place on the following Thursday afternoon, in the courtyard of our old synagogue. Dayan Gestettner would marry us. It was one week since the Jews of my town had been concentrated into a ghetto, surrounded by a high fence.

On Wednesday night I stole out of the asylum. Like a criminal I scurried from house to house – yet all I was going to do was to follow the yearning of my heart, to marry the one I loved. I walked around the ghetto, and about midnight I climbed over the fence. But twenty-one-year-old greenhorn that I was, I did not realize that night that I was clambering back into the Middle Ages.

When I was in my teens and went to Hebrew class, I learnt a great deal about the ghettos of the past. To me then the ghetto of the Middle Ages meant not only degradation but also a great and important phase in Jewish history. I learned that during the periods when my people were left in peace the ghetto was a pleasant place, where family life flourished alongside the study of the Talmud. I also learned that it was within the walls of the ghetto that much beautiful and important literature was created. Dreams and fantasies were also part of the atmosphere within the closed walls, dreams about Eretz Israel, the long lost State of Israel, and of the coming of the Messiah, when the world would cease to suffer. Branded with the yellow star, my ancestors had spoken about the Jordan and Jerusalem with as much familiarity as if they themselves had only recently returned from the

Holy Land. And because as an oppressed group they were weak and could count on help from no one, they turned with fanatical belief to "our Father in heaven," the only help, the only hope in human misery.

How different that ghetto was from the one I faced on that critical Wednesday night in the year of 1944. Now the eyes into which I looked mirrored only horror and fear. Six thousand people were crammed into a space inadequate for even two thousand. There was no privacy. Whole families, sometimes twenty people or more were crowded into a single room.

This ghetto was a part of the oldest, poorest part of my town, and had only a few streets. During the day thousands were out on these streets, listening to the ever-increasing rumors. Food was scarce, so most of the time people were hungry. Hunger, desperation and fear made people intolerant of each other, and there were quarrels about the most irrelevant trifles. Husbands and wives who had lived quietly together for years now blamed each other for "wrongs" done long ago, and accused each other of things that were seldom true. The old despised the young and accused them of bad manners, when they themselves were quite unable to set a good example. The young hated the old and blamed them for the tragedy that had befallen Jewry, saying that they were decadent and spineless and urging them to fight the Germans. Everyone urged everyone else to do something, and in the meantime the secret police were beating and torturing people at the rooms of the Jewish Community Centre to force them to disclose their hidden "treasure."

The only ones who accepted this tragic fate without a murmur were the long-bearded Chassidic Jews, who turned their eyes towards the sky, to the same clear, eternal blue to which their persecuted ancestors had raised their eyes throughout history. They did not rebel, they did not accuse, they did not bully. They prayed: *"Avinu*

*Malkenu, hotonu lefonecho"* (Our Father, Our King, we have sinned against Thee). They had a power within themselves that had made the Germans powerless; they possessed a greatness that made me feel small and insignificant. I understood then how we have managed to withstand the persecution of the centuries. It was not because of our wealth, not because of our great scientists and artists, who so often remained Jews only in name. It was because of these long-bearded men, rich in spirit and poor in earthly possessions, who studied the holy books day and night throughout thousands of years; who believed every word of the Torah, the Old Testament; who heard the voice of God in their dreams, and who could bring color and gaiety into their prayers, and joy into their communication with God.

To the rest of us, the ghetto meant shame and suffering. We wept because we had lost our shops, our books, our paintings, our houses and money. We swore, when no one heard, that one day we would repay with interest the damage done to us. But these old men, sitting in the courtyard of the synagogue, taught that "Judgment is only in the hand of the Lord."

These were also the Yiddish words of Dayan Gestettner, who married us on Thursday afternoon as we stood under the canopy.

"Do not be afraid," he said. "They cannot harm us, only kill us; they can hurt the body, but not the soul. It is body and soul that is united in marriage. And the Judgment for all wrong-doing and sin is in the hand of the Lord."

Then Eva lifted her veil and we kissed. Our friends shed a few tears and, not believing their own words, wished us "good luck."

Eva's family had managed to empty a room for us. As a surprise Eva had hung a picture of my mother on the wall – a portrait painted by a well-known artist about the time of my birth, which used to hang in Father's study. It was a part of my childhood. Wedding night in the ghetto.

We huddled together in bed, both crying, both comforting each other: "Don't cry, don't cry...."

"This isn't how we used to imagine it, is it?"

"No my love, it isn't."

A patrol passed in the street, the boots of the gendarmes, those Hungarian monsters, reverberating on the pavement.

Trembling, our embrace tightened.

"The Jews are asleep," one voice shouted across to the other side of the street, to his companion.

"Before long they're going to sleep even deeper," bawled the other. Both of them guffawed.

"I'm scared, Jancsi."

"Don't be afraid, my darling."

"I'm afraid that I'll lose you...."

"Don't be afraid, my sweetheart."

"You won't ever leave me, will you?"

"I shall never leave you."

And then our desperate, parched lips met, shutting out the world, the Middle Ages, the twentieth century. No more ghetto or yellow star, no Hitler, no deportations. Nothing existed but the two of us, two young hearts beating in the dark, locked close to one another.

At dawn we set out for our honeymoon; the cock had not yet crowed when we were out in the street. Eva's skirt got caught up on the fence and tore. Down the familiar alleyways and streets we crept, towards the asylum. Would they admit Eva? Or would they throw her out into the street? Would they allow us to steal a little happiness in the midst of this vast unhappiness?

We were given separate rooms. But at night we met in the garden. The ground was warm and, like our eyes, wet with dew. The dawns were sweet and sad. And weary, too.

Then one night, one of the male nurses, a Nazi, discovered our secret and from that time we were in constant anxiety of being reported to the Gestapo. We did not even think of the (unwitting) possibility that the nurse was only a Peeping Tom, who derived a certain amount of enjoyment from our unconscious exhibition, and who would willingly let us carry on. During those days we smelt danger everywhere, so we decided it would be safer for Eva to leave.

But the loneliness that I experienced after her departure became intolerable. I could perhaps have escaped, but life would not have been worth while without Eva or my family. So after some restless days (and restless nights) I decided to go back to the ghetto and share my people's fate. I had learnt during those days I had been alone that to perish amongst the people you love is better than to live isolated in the hostile world.

On the July 3, 1944, we were taken from the ghetto to a factory, an abandoned brickyard. That night, together with many thousands of other Jews, we lay in the yard of the factory, awaiting sunrise and deportation from our homeland. And there, for the last time, we embraced.

The stars burned in the night sky. The smiling moon looked down upon the earth: short-sighted, she could not see what was happening below.

In the morning, with whips and truncheons, they herded us into cattle trucks. I could clearly hear the click of the lock as it was placed on the door of the truck. We were sealed in.

# CHAPTER II

As I recalled that nightmare three-day journey which bridged the abyss between two worlds, the horror of the past flooded back with renewed intensity, like the pain from a sudden blow that reopens a slowly healing wound. I had mounted the train of death wearing European clothes, a European man; I alighted at the other end a dazed creature of Auschwitz.

The air was oppressive. People were lying on top of each other like sardines in a tin. In the first few hours we did not feel the melting heat, but by the time dawn had passed and the sun shone on to the walls of the truck, sweat was coursing down my forehead in large drops.

"What will happen now, Jancsi?"

I glanced at Eva's narrow little face. Only her blue eyes seemed alive in it.

"I don't know, dear. I don't know. I don't know what will happen. If this is only the beginning, what will the rest of it be like?"

I looked around at the eighty-three people crammed together in the sealed cattle truck. Next to us a young woman was giving suck to her baby, but the milk seemed to have disappeared from her breasts. The little creature was crying.

"What are you thinking of, darling?" Eva looked at me with her large eyes.

"I am thinking of life, of how I used to believe in humanity. Well, now I have got the answer as to whether it was worth believing in."

The train, still on Hungarian soil, raced forward with its human cargo. Sitting down on the trunks which were

13

threatening to fall over any moment, I leaned my head against the side of the truck, and closed my eyes. Eva curled up next to me. The weary breathing of my neighbors sounded in my ears. Unbelievable chaos reigned in the truck. It was seven hours since the train had pulled out of the station; it had run without a stop. They had not given us any water yet. I pressed my face against the iron bars of the window and drew a deep breath, and with it the colors of reality seemed to brighten a little. The people around me became the people of my childhood again. I remembered them in the streets of my town, or standing in the entrance of their shops. Some were rich, others just managed to exist. They had all grown up with me, so that I could not recognize the changes wrought on their faces by time. Amongst them was a married woman who had had an affair; everyone knew about it except her husband. Now they traveled together in the truck, pressed close to one another – the husband and the wife and the lover. Another was a violinist. Perched on his violin case, he stared into nothingness. Once I had heard him play, under the brilliant light of chandeliers. And next to me was Eva, panting for air – my first great love.

I remembered our first trysts at her Grannie's house, the stolen kisses which tasted so sweet. Shortsighted and hard of hearing, Eva's Grannie was ideally suited for the task of Cupid. Grannie, too, was lying here, only a few yards away from us.

Poor old Grannie. She used to sit there in her armchair during the winter afternoons, dozing off, starting up now and again. How we used to bamboozle the old lady! Bat-like her eyes would turn towards us (she could hardly see a thing) as she asked: "Still busy sewing, my girlie?" Then Eva would free herself from my embrace and answer innocently: "Of course I'm sewing, Grannie. What else could I be doing?" Grannie was fond of me, too. At teatime she would tell Eva: "Go on, girlie, make some coffee for the gentleman." Time had stopped for Grannie, or rather time had stopped *within* her. For years she had seen nothing, heard nothing. Behind her veiled eyes, no longer reached by the radiance of the sun, memories kept watch over the sunlight of the past; in her ears memories stood guard over the voice of bygone years. She visualized the world as though nothing had changed during the decades. Her manner of speech was quaintly old-fashioned. Often for this reason she had been the object of our ill-bred ridicule. Now Grannie was lying on the floor of the truck, not knowing where she was, knowing nothing of the horrors which were taking place in the world. She believed that she was still at home, just a little giddy on account of some slight indisposition. "Go on, girlie, make some coffee for the gentleman!" But today Grannie's coffee failed to arrive. She began to chide Eva: "What a badly brought up girl you are! Your mind seems to be on some silly nonsense all the time. Well, if you're so lazy, then at least go and fetch me a glass of water. Can't you hear what I'm asking?"

In the silence that followed I could hear Eva crying softly by my side. My eyes, too, were wet.

"What a naughty girl you are! Can't you hear your Grannie is thirsty?!" Helplessly she groped around her. "Are you still here, young man?"

"Here I am, Madam," I yelled loud enough for her to hear me. I stroked her hand, and the old lady's features relaxed.

"I do hope, my dear young man, you won't mind if I ask you to bring me some water? If you would be good enough to go straight through that door to the kitchen. Well, now, if you'd be good enough to turn left you'll find the tap there. The glasses are on your right, on the shelf."

I crawled over to her and gently caressed her grey hair. For a long time, a very long time she stared ahead in utter incomprehension. Then she closed her sightless eyes.

It was close on evening. Dense shadows were gathering in the truck.

"We're in the Carpathians now," said Eva. I looked out of the small, iron-barred window. Faintly the last rays of the sun shone on to the mighty, somber slopes. We reached the frontier by night, where all the trucks were unsealed and a high-ranking German officer announced that we would be taken to a camp in Germany. At our place of arrival warm food would be awaiting us, he told us. They could not provide water for us here, but later we should be given plenty of that as well. The words sounded reassuring but no one believed them. We had learnt from past experience that one could not believe the Germans.

Nothing much happened while the train was waiting at the frontier station. As long as Hungarian voices could be heard outside the truck things were still all right. But soon after the train started rolling again somebody said: "We are just crossing the frontier."

The words haunted the truck as though uttered by a ghost. In a far corner someone started humming the Hungarian national anthem. A country ejects its own citizens over the border – and in the moment of leaving her they hum the national anthem! But nobody interrupted the tune. We all shared the sentiment. We listened to the anthem and said farewell – to Hungary, to our native land, to our grandparents' graves, to the place of our first love, to the land of our agony and our delights. It was a though we felt in our very souls how hard it was to tear ourselves away from the dark landscape and the mountains which seemed to draw us back to them. Then fear took hold of us.

Strange phantoms were hovering in the dark; at first slowly, then gradually faster they trembled before my eyes. I did not dare to move. It was as if the ghosts of a dead man and a dead woman were seeking one another across the crowded truck. I had never believed in the supernatural; I used to think that spiritualists were harmless crackpots. Now, with bated breath, half-demented, I watched the moving shadows which were approaching me.

A strange young woman whom I could not recognize in the darkness caught my hand, trembling. I did not understand who she was, what she wanted of me. But I, too, gripped her hand as in a vice. Then I put my arm around her waist and drew her towards me. I needed her feverish lips and kisses, her writhing body, to shut out my fears. I did not know who I was or where I was. I had but one desire – a desire for this unknown woman. Screaming, I pressed against her breasts as I peered fearfully into the dark to see whether the phantoms were any nearer. Even with my eyes closed I could see them before me: hissing, horrible, eerie. As I felt her hot body against mine I asked her: "Can you see them? Can you see those shadows?" She made no reply. The more I was afraid the tighter I held her. I hardly noticed that everybody else in the truck was crying, delirious, groaning, trembling and writhing.

"I was never yours before, Feri," the strange woman said, breathing with difficulty. "Darling Feri, I never gave myself to you," she groaned in my arms. "I wanted you so much, but I was afraid of having a baby, afraid of suffering and even of myself." Her voice glowed with passion. "Come, Feri, my darling. Hold me, hold me tight. Oh, how it hurts – but how good it is when you hold me!"

I came to my senses. As though murdering each other, people were screaming in the truck.

"Eva, is that you?" I felt the unknown body. "Eva, Eva! Oh, my God, what has happened to me?"

For a moment the moon shone through the window into the train. Eva was lying in a stupor some distance away. I looked behind me to see whom I had been embracing. I had never seen her before. "I must be going mad." Again I was overcome by giddiness. "No, I must not let this get the better of me. I am strong, stronger than any ghost. I must control myself."

I spent the rest of that night between the agony of sleep and the agony of consciousness. At sunrise the train was rattling through somber, mountainous country. As I glanced through the barred window I saw an armed SS guard – the first SS soldier I had yet encountered. He had a dark, bestial face.

Someone clambered on to his knees beside me. He had been an architect in my town, but that single night had changed him so much that I hardly recognized him. Trembling, he gripped the iron bars of the window.

"I implore you, sir, let me have some water. My wife is feeling ill," he begged the guard.

A broad grin spread across the face of the SS man. As if to scare a child, he suddenly took the automatic rifle from his shoulder.

"It's water you want, eh? Wouldn't it be better if I gave you a bullet instead?" He laughed coarsely.

The architect forced a smile, thinking that the SS man was joking. "No, please, I beg you, just a little water – just a small sip for my wife. She might die, God help her."

"She might die?" asked the SS man. "Might she now? Jews don't die; they just peg out. The way you're going to right now...." There was a quiet little click. It took me a few seconds to realize that the soldier wearing the emblem of skull and crossbones had pulled the trigger of his automatic rifle.

A great hiccough shook the architect's body, as a red patch appeared under his left shoulder. The patch began to spread.

Apart from me no one had noticed yet that he had been shot. Slowly he slid to the ground, and his blood splashed over me as I put my arms around his waist. Gradually his eyes glazed; he began to gasp. It was the first time in my life that I had witnessed one human being kill another. Now I saw how simple it is to end a man's life. A click, a few gasps, and it is all over.

Only now did the sick woman catch sight of her husband collapsing into a pool of blood. "Karoly, Karoly, what's the matter with you?" With a tremendous effort she crawled over the people in her way, oblivious of the bodies on which she was treading, and threw herself over her husband's corpse. "Wake up, Karoly!" Screaming, she began to shake him. "Wake up! It's me – Lina, your own Lina, who loves you." Then suddenly she stopped. For a moment she clung to her husband's body as though crying. Then, bloodstained from his wounds, with fear in her lifeless eyes, she rolled off into the surrounding mass of people.

Outside the truck the trees were swaying in the wind, and here and there among the mountains a lake glittered in the sun. The sky was alive with wonderful colors. Everything outside was as glorious as if all were well in the world. But in the small world within the truck the tragedy of the architect and his wife was merely the prelude to others.

An old man was the next to suffer calamity. When he saw that the Germans would not give us any water he thought he might make more room for himself by suspending the empty water bucket, by means of some string, from a nail that jutted out of the roof of the truck. And to create yet a little more room for his neighbors, he put another two buckets into the first one. Like a pendulum the pile of buckets swung on the thin string. It occurred to nobody that they might fall. Towards evening, while the train was running through a lovely landscape, it happened. The knot gave way; the three buckets, one inside the other, crashed down on the old man's skull and split it open. In an instant he was covered with blood. The unfortunate old man did not realize what had happened; he kept on touching his skull as, with protruding eyes, he looked around him. His appearance was quite ghastly. Some of the people burst into hysterical laughter at the dreadful sight; others started to shriek. Then the old man started to wander about the truck as if looking for something, and I knew that he had gone mad. He stopped in front of me and stared at me. His demented gaze pierced into my heart.

"Well, well, I'll eat my hat if this isn't our budding advocate! When are we going home, my little lawyer?" And as if he were merely strolling down the street in our home town, he walked on, with a final "My regards to Daddy, little lawyer."

"Little lawyer"... how well I remembered this old man. As a child I used to love the jokes he always cracked with me. I remembered how he used to hand me a toffee each time we met in the street. Since my father was a lawyer, I became automatically the "little lawyer." "Well, what are you going to be when you grow up? Another little lawyer perhaps?"

I remembered, too, the old man's daughter, Lola, who had experienced difficulty in hooking a husband – in spite of her considerable dowry. It was reputed that Lola's mouth had a rather unpleasant taste. No one would kiss her a second time. At any rate, that was the story I had heard from a cousin who was articled to my father. The old man had a son, too, who had always stammered and who was not quite right in the head, either. He had a compulsion to sing whatever he wanted to say, with special tunes to match different words. If he wanted a glass of water he had to sing for it, otherwise it would have taken him hours to come to the end of his request. Now the family was all together in the truck.

The boy was singing away at the moment. His words – "Daaaaadddy's heaaaaad is aaawfully bloooody" – went to the tune of a popular hit song. Lola (who had eventually married a melancholy, sick man who, she confessed, had embraced her only twice in their married life yet who had managed to beget a child), lay twitching by her mother's side, choking, blue in the face.

I turned away from this terrible sight. My nerves were strained to breaking point, and I needed all my strength to control myself.

It began to rain, and the rain water trickled down from the roof of the truck. I put out a small tin mug between the bars to catch it, but in the darkness I could not see where the water was running off. I held the cup out blindly, while occasional gusts of wind blew in through the window, splashing the rain into my face and helping to overcome the numbness which had all but conquered me.

The whole truck was now running amok. Thirst and the lack of air had robbed people of their senses. They were tearing and stabbing at one another; their screams echoed through the dark. At the first station at which the train halted for a little while I called out through the window to the SS guard in front of the truck:

"People are killing one another. They have gone completely mad. Would you please ask the commander in charge of the train for a torch so that we can see what is happening, and some rope to tie up those who are raving mad? And I beg you, get us some water!"

"No water," he said. For a few moments he disappeared, then he came back bringing the torch and the rope I had requested. I turned on the torch and shone it into the darkness. A terrible sight met my eyes. One man was gesticulating wildly with a pocketknife in his hand, stabbing people to right and left in a lunatic abandon. Many people lay on the floor, their bodies bloody and writhing. An attack of hysteria seemed to have swept through the truck, infecting one person after another. I saw that this frenzied violence might well lead to murder if nothing were done to stop it. A few young men were lying not far from me. I pulled them up from the floor and shone the torch in their eyes.

"Listen to me. Our lives are in danger – these madmen could easily kill us in the dark. We must tie them up."

I had never before taken part in an enterprise as dangerous as this. One after the other we tied up the madmen; each time the rope grew taut on people to whom I myself was tied by memories. There they lay, unhappy human beings transformed by thirst into madmen and murderers.

The sound of a violin reached my ear – our violinist was playing Paganini. The energy, fury and exaltation of the music cut across the maddened night. The lad's father, a frail little merchant whose voice had hardly ever been heard from one year to the other, was now preaching at the top of his voice:

"Almighty God, why have you done this to us? Have you no heart, no feelings? Have you no eyes to see with? Have you no ears to hear us with? You are wicked, O Lord, as wicked as man."

A doctor kept on repeating endlessly, "The higher the temperature rises, the better it kills the bacteria." Then he turned to me: "Isn't that so, sir?"

Around me people were raging, yelling, screaming. I told myself that this night must mark a turning point, that if we survived this one night we were over the worst of it. It was only a matter of one night. For this reason I would not allow myself to drop in a swoon on the floor of the truck, I would not let go of myself. I wanted to live. And the train ran rattling on and on.

From outside the wind whistled through the truck. Far away on the edge of the sky a dirty grey stripe began to thicken. It was dawn. The smell of rain dilated my nostrils. It would probably be another grey, overcast day. What would the day bring, and the day after that? What would the weeks and the months bring? What would happen if the war went on for a long time? What would happen to us then?

The outlines of the trees were already discernible as the forests glided past us. The train was running towards the rising sun. I was thirsty. How wonderful it would be to open the door of the truck, leap out on to the grass glistening with raindrops and lick up the water from the ground. How good it would be to step out into this grey and meaningless morning twilight, to walk across the soggy earth, arrive at a well and drink, drink, drink of the water and then with open arteries stare at the grey sky through the empty eyes of the dead. I was alone. This frequently recurring thought made me shudder. Everybody to whom I belonged was either unconscious or dead. Eva, too, was lying in a coma by my feet. And then I saw my mother's face approaching from the distance.

"You, Mother, you alone stand by me in this hour of need. Once upon a time, long ago, as you lay on your sickbed under the pale light of the bedside lamp, you told me: "If ever you really need me, Jancsi, you will see me standing by your side, even if I have to leave you soon. Death is a mighty master but one cannot kill love." "Mother, dear, I feel that in some mysterious way you are here with me this morning. Open the sealed doors; let me out into the open air. I cannot hold out much longer."

They brought no water. At each station we waited for water to come – the water of life – but in vain. All was quiet in the truck which now looked like a butcher's shop. I bent down to Eva. I opened her mouth and breathed some air into it; with my dry tongue I licked her forehead to try and impart some moisture to her. In vain. Too late now. Too late for everything. I could not even escape any longer; for I did not have sufficient strength left in me to drag myself up to the barred window. The night had passed, but the suffering and terror remained. Eva had come round, but was too weak to speak. She could only look at me with large, terrified eyes.

A pain almost akin to pleasure shot through me. Slowly I grew dizzy. I could feel my temples throbbing wildly, the veins standing out on my arms. Then everything went dark.

The sun scorched down on a world which was turning in a confused mass around me. Black spots were dancing in front of my eyes, and the longing for water stabbed through my body.

"Water!"

It was the only word, the only thought I could hold on to.

Down the long road leading from the station a line of people were dragging along with slow, weary steps. Here and there a face seemed to bear some obscure message which I could not read....

I had arrived, in July, 1944, at the concentration camp of Auschwitz.

# CHAPTER III

We stood in the courtyard in brilliant sunshine, each one dressed in a garment that resembled pyjamas. Dogs were barking in the distance; somewhere a gong sounded. As soon as everybody had finished in the showers, we started off. Here and there through the windows of the barracks we saw eyes peering at us, black-rimmed and sunken. They were the eyes of men and women, half-naked, who dragged their bodies along the ground. But after we had passed through the big iron gates the scene changed suddenly. On both sides of the long road green trees swayed in the breeze, carefully kept gardens smiled in front of the barracks, and farther off neat ponds reflected the blue sky in their shining ripples. Men and women in smart clothes were walking along the road. At first sight this road reminded me of some seaside resort, with its shady trees and smiling gardens. The sound of jazz music drifted from the barracks. Once again I felt dizzy, as I failed to comprehend the contrast between this and the world behind the gates.

Our guards drove us into an enormous barrack. The music, still audible from the neighboring buildings, lent an air of unreality to the scene: it was like a circus. As soon as we had all arrived a man in a zebra-suit (that was the name we gave to our prison clothes) stepped on to a chair in the middle of the barrack.

"Attention! Listen carefully. Keep your ears open – I'm not going to repeat myself. First of all, this camp is called Birkenau. It belongs to the Lager of Auschwitz. Birkenau consists of two parts: in one they work, in the other they don't. They are better off in the working camp:

25

there each person sleeps on a separate wooden bunk, has a separate blanket and, of course, gets more to eat. The other part, where we are, is bad. Here you don't have to work. And so you starve. No bed, no blanket, not even straw to sleep on. You must sleep on the floor and huddle together to keep each other warm. Providing you can sleep that way at all," he added with a grin. "But Birkenau isn't meant to be a summer resort. If you should fall ill, there is no doctor, or medicine. Sick people soon kick the bucket here." He paused for a moment. The howling of dogs and the sound of a gong could be heard in the distance, mingling with the music. Then he went on:

"The food is not fit for pigs – but anyway you won't last long on this kind of diet. The tea will make you vomit and feel dizzy. And at night you will have some visitors – you'll find out about that for yourselves. Just one more thing: inside the camp the *Altesters* (heads) call the tune, and anyone who disobeys them is going to peg out pretty quickly. You can see the rank of the various guards on their armbands. "LA" means *Lagerältester* [head of the camp]. Where the prisoners are concerned, he is the boss in Birkenau. You will have the pleasure of meeting him later. The barrack commander is marked "A" – that means simply *Altester*. When you go to work, you will meet guards who carry different markings. *Vorarbeiter* means foreman: if he knocks you about, well, you just shut up. "*Kapo*" stands for *Kameradpolizei* (prisoner functionary); these are higher even than the *Vorarbeiter*. Before them, too, you keep your mouths shut. And last but not least, before me. I am *Ältester* of this barrack, Block 17.

"Well, now," he continued with great relish, "first of all you will be x-rayed. That'll show up anything you might try to conceal. If we find anything valuable hidden on anybody, we beat him to death then and there. Like this..." He jumped off the chair, dragged an old man from the queue and with his stick thrashed him mercilessly until the wretched creature could no longer move. Then, as if nothing had happened, he stepped on to the chair once again. The battered body of the old man lay on the ground before him as he continued with unperturbed calm.

"So, if you don't want to come to the same end, you had better give up your hidden valuables quickly. Then you can bloody well sit down where you are. And don't you dare make too much noise: I can't bear that rotten lingo of yours. Besides, I loathe you Hungarian mob. *Verstanden?* (Understood?)"

Of course there was no grain of truth in the story about the x-ray. All this Polish *Blockältester* wanted was to grab anything valuable that might have been hidden in our shoes, in order to sell it to the SS men in exchange for some food. But the men, dazed and exhausted as they were, could not think straight. One after the other they stepped forward to the chair, tore open the soles of their shoes and surrendered the things they had hidden there, their last remaining possessions: small diamonds, gold rings, bank notes. All their other belongings had already been taken from them long ago. Some of their things they had had to leave in the railway wagons; others remained in the clothes they had shed at the baths.

The *Blockältester* smiled with a satisfied expression as he pocketed the things. Then he jumped off the chair and with a swaggering gait walked to his special compartment at the front part of the barrack.

Unable to move any more, people dropped to the concrete floor and lay there, and soon the barrack was filled with the sound of groans and heavy breathing. The sun had set. Beyond the barrack an enormous chimney belched a mixture of flames and smoke into the sky. I groped my way to the door for a breath of air. From afar there came an incessant howling of dogs, ringing of gongs, and the muted scream of hooters. From a very great distance (but maybe I only imagined this) the weeping of women and children was carried to me on the wind. And against the sky the fire rose higher all the time, dyeing everything around the color of blood.

A few days after our arrival a slip of paper drifted in over the fence. It came from the women's side of the camp.

Someone called: "Heimler, Heimler, is there a bastard called Heimler here?"

Then I read the note.

"To Eugene Heimler. Your wife died this afternoon after an attack of dysentery. It was her last wish that I should let you know." Then came a signature, which I have forgotten.

The days which followed merged into an indistinct mass. I had completely lost my sense of time. Time in Auschwitz was not divided into minutes; the week did not consist of seven days. The only measure of time was one's ebbing vitality.

Back home each hour used to have its own hue and flavor. In the morning my father would stretch in his bed. I could hear his quiet yawn from next door. From the kitchen would come the clanging of pots and pans, as the noises of the morning filtered in from the staircase. Sleepy-eyed, my sister would rush in to breakfast: "Oh, God, half-past seven, I'll be late for school." Slowly the morning light flowed in through the curtains, washing the shadows of night from the furniture. In my father's office, the typewriter would start up; round the corner, the blacksmith would be at his anvil.

In Auschwitz the sun rose crimson behind the electrified wire fence. The air was cold, yet it failed to bring color into faces still drawn by the torments of the night. In the narrow yard between the barracks it mattered so little whether the sun was rising or setting – nights and days alike meant only weariness and exhaustion.

How clearly I could review the past from this cold and forbidding world of the barracks! I heard voices; fragments of insignificant conversations emerged in my memory while they were dishing out the uneatable concoction called "lunch." Five of us ate off one plate. If one of the five took one bite more than his due, we flew at one another and then literally licked up the food that spilled on the floor. There were even some who killed in their hunger. I had known these people at home. Once they had been respectable, cultured citizens, members of charitable societies and select clubs.

At home, lunch used to be ready at noon. While Mother served the meal, Father would bury himself in the paper.

"Here we sit happily, while all these horrors are taking place over there," he said one day, pointing at the page.

"Are you thinking of Germany?" asked Mother. He nodded but said nothing. Then, with a little sigh, he started ladling out the soup. A wasp kept knocking against the window-pane. My sister opened the window and the silly creature joyously flew out into the open. It was an oppressive afternoon, heavy with an approaching storm. The dull roll of thunder shook the far horizon.

"Yes, here we sit and eat our fill, while a nation is being locked into a cage. Well, don't we all share the guilt of it?" he demanded, still following the same train of thought. "However, what we say won't help much."

It was as if I were seeing the past reflected in a broken mirror. In the shattered fragments the world lived on. For the fragments of a mirror do not die.

My brain was humming as I lay in the slowly narrowing shadow of the barracks. During the hours of the morning they cast a wide shadow; but as the sun rose higher in the sky the shadows became ever narrower. I was giddy from the bromide which they mixed into our tea. At last the rays of the sun were pouring down upon me with scorching intensity. Blood-red crystals danced in front of my closed eyes; small rings of all hues of the rainbow flooded my vision. I imagined myself back home again, in the familiar old streets. I waved to someone, but the next moment the image faded away. Tatters of gipsy melodies wailed in my ears and sank back into the abyss of oblivion before I could recognize them.

In the barracks which rose dark and forbidding on the other side of the road a colony of gypsies had settled. Their "Aryan" origin entitled them to special privileges: men and women could live together and even have children in the camp. In the years since they had been dragged here, little harm had been done to them. They lazed about in the elegant clothes of which we had been robbed by the SS; they did not have to work; in fact, they enjoyed quite a good time. All of us were very scared of the gypsies. They were dangerous: whenever they had a chance, they knocked us about.

I lay there next to the electrified fence, on the opposite side of the road to the gypsies, growing more and more lethargic. It was a strange kind of numbness. My eyelids felt heavy as lead, my limbs as though they were paralyzed. With closed eyes, I lay inert in the sunshine. The noises of the camp sounded fainter and fainter. All at once everything became utterly silent. The suddenness with which this occurred threw me into a panic. Around me and within me, the moment became dumb and motionless. And then, in the petrified darkness, it seemed as if someone started to walk towards me from a long way off. I longed to cry out, to scream, to break the silence with my voice, and the darkness, too, and to drive away the one who seemed to be approaching. But no sound came from my lips. The Unknown came nearer and nearer. I could almost hear his silent steps, the rustle of his clothes. "What do you want?" the words shaped themselves in my mind. "What do you want from me? Why won't you let me see your face?" And then, as if he understood my terror, he leaned forward and seemed to whisper in my ear: "After the evening roll-call get away from Barrack No. 17. It is dangerous there. Dangerous. Danger!" His words reached me indistinct and distorted, as if echoed by dark mountains and divided by valleys across thousands of miles, as if in a dream.

I do not know whether it was only minutes or whole hours that passed before the darkness began to recede. I opened my eyes as the heat of the sun struck me with blinding force. I could not comprehend what had happened. I tried to stand up but my limbs seemed to be chained to the ground by fetters of lead. I leaned my head on my clenched fists. With the utmost concentration I tried to remember what had happened. But I could hear nothing except that unidentified voice: "It is dangerous. Danger."

While the whispered warning churned ceaselessly in my mind, I recalled a night in which a dream brought me a similar vision. Was there any connection between the two? The dream occurred on the night of March 18, 1944. I dreamed that I was being transported somewhere on a lorry. Others were also in the lorry. The sky above was slowly turning the color of blood: there was something strange even in the smell of the wind. The lorry took us to the military parade ground, where once I had learned to shoot. In my dream the field appeared deserted and terrifyingly silent. As we jumped off the lorries I suddenly froze with fright: a soldier wearing a swastika armband emerged from the driver's seat. With the others I was lined up in a long queue; among them I recognized childhood playfellows, friends, relations. The crowd started to march towards a freshly dug pit. Beneath the blood-red sun the blade of a guillotine fell repeatedly with a dull thud, and into the pit in their thousands rolled an unending tide of human beings. Long after the blade had fallen, the blood-stained headless corpses were still writhing.

In the meantime the soldier who had emerged from the driver's seat walked past the people in the queue, looking everyone in the eye. Whoever appeared intimidated by his glance was made to fall out of line and was directed towards the pit. As he approached me in my turn icy perspiration covered my brow – I felt that I was living through the most critical moments of my life. At last he was standing in front of me. His cold eyes bored into mine, trying to hypnotize me to death. I knew that this was a battle of wills between us, and that if but once I was caught in the blue whirlpool of death in his eyes, I was lost. For a second I was winning, and then I felt that my strength was ebbing, that despite my will I was on the way to the pit in which heaved the dark sea of doomed bodies. There was a shovel in my hand, the kind that grave-diggers use in the cemetery. Slowly the thought came to me: "You must die, you will die – but why die alone? The shovel in your hand is a weapon. You still have the strength to strike. If you must die, make certain that this murderer dies too." I turned back, lifted up my shovel and with upraised arms ran towards him. Suddenly everything appeared to become formless, and fear shot through me. It even seemed as if this man, whose eyes had radiated such terror, was not a man at all but a figure of clay. With a face of clay he turned towards the sun which was setting behind the hills. For a moment I thought that he wanted to lure me into a trap, and that he had already fired the bullet carrying my death, but when my frenzied rush had brought me up to him I saw that it was indeed only an unarmed figure of clay which stared witlessly into the void. My onslaught was checked; my arm, raised to attack, was lowered without effect. I woke up. Looking at my watch, I saw that it was 3:30 in the morning.

The following morning, March 19, when my sister, deathly pale announced to us the news that at 3:30 that morning the Germans had crossed the border and occupied our country, I was not even surprised.

On the afternoon of my warning vision in the camp, a sudden commotion started up during the customary roll-call (the so-called *"Appel"*). The road was emptied of traffic, sirens hooted, gongs were struck.

The SS patrol on motorcycles had arrived before our barrack. Their leader, a tall, blond officer, yelled from afar: *"Hauptschwein, antreten!"* (Chief of pigs, line up!) With trembling limbs and knees knocking, the barrack commander moved towards him. "Enough – stop there. Don't come any nearer, you filthy beast!" the SS man shouted at him, and went on to order him to report the number of "carcasses" – that is, sick people – in the barrack. The SS man then started off towards the queues to ascertain personally the number of those unfit to work.

As the SS officer drew nearer, a flash of recognition struck me: this was the main figure in my dream on the night of the German invasion. The people who were there in my dream were with me now; I recognized the weird, dream-like atmosphere. I began to shake with fear. Reality and dream were no longer distinct from each other. I knew what was coming. I knew that he would stand before me with eyes in which one might drown, and set me on the road to death. And while all this flashed through me, someone leaned towards me and whispered

33

in my ear the same words I had heard from the apparition that morning: "After the roll call get away from Barrack No. 17. Danger...."

The SS officer was now standing in front of me. I felt that even the wind had stopped blowing. In a thousandth fraction of that second strange images flitted through my mind. I felt as if I could see beyond the barracks, across space and time. Past, present and future converged to a point within me. He looked at me, and as if mesmerized I looked back deep into his eyes. I do not know how long we were staring at one another. I do not know how long he stood before me.

A harsh shout brought me back to my senses. The *Appel* was over. People were slowly dispersing. I knew that something was about to happen, that I had to do something. Half-conscious, I stumbled towards the electrified fence.

A long ditch ran between the electric fence and the back entrance of the barracks. If someone could no longer bear his dreadful existence and deliberately touched the live wire or chanced to rush against it in a fit of nerves, his body, struck dead in an instant, fell into the ditch and lay there until the "Sondercommando" came to take it to the crematorium. It was in this ditch that I took refuge after the *Appel* was over. Feigning death, I lay there motionless. Yet I did not understand myself why I did so. Some unknown power seemed to have benumbed my senses, holding my thoughts and movements in suspension.

I had been lying there for a long time, watched only by the glassy stare of several corpses, when suddenly I became aware of a loud rumbling. Till then I seemed to have been in a coma, but this noise brought me back to full consciousness. I recognized it immediately – SS lorries were rolling into the camp. Almost at once they pulled up sharply before Barrack No. 17. The night was dark; only the headlamps of the lorries lit the scene. I held my breath and listened. Curt words of command were clearly audible. I knew what they meant: no one might leave the barracks.

With rifle butts, whips and bare fists they goaded my comrades from the barrack into the lorries. Now and again a shot echoed through the night. The minutes seemed endlessly long. Suddenly I sensed that someone was approaching the ditch.

"Well, what are we to do with these carcasses?" I could recognize the SS soldier by his voice as he addressed his companion. I did not dare to move my head or to look up out of the ditch. I lay there, my arms spread like the other dead bodies. His torch wavered over the corpses. "Look, that one's still moving," he yelled. "He's moving, the stinking carcass." Cold sweat broke out all over me. I knew that his machine gun would be trained towards the ditch. I longed to cry out "No, not this way. I don't want to die like this." But I was paralyzed. A single shot rang out, followed by a dull groan, then quiet again. He must have finished off someone not yet quite dead – perhaps one of those who had been thrown into the ditch in the afternoon after having been nearly beaten to death.

Minutes passed.

Then the steps receded. They would probably make a special trip for the corpses in the ditch later on.

It was only now that I became aware of the screams and cries that filled the night. One after the other the lorries started off, loaded with human cargo for their fiery destination. The whispered stories that I had heard from the older prisoners about the gas chambers now hit me with dreadful reality. It seemed to be true after all – a thing which even here had seemed unbelievable.

Slowly I lifted up my head as the last of the lorries was passing through the camp gates with its wailing load. Barrack No. 17 gaped wide open in terrible emptiness. I had to get away from it, forget I ever belonged to it, get into some other barrack.

"Away, away from here.... Quickly, quickly...."

On all fours I began to crawl along the ditch. I knocked into dead bodies – I climbed over them. My hands were smeared with their blood. Each movement had to be made with care lest I touch the electrified fence. The search-lights on the watchtowers scanned the night, sweeping round the camp. As the beam came towards me I froze on the ground, arms spread out, eyes wide open, until the light had passed me. On, on.... The fire of the crematorium flared up, higher and higher. As though propelled by some superhuman force, I crawled from barrack to barrack.

Near one of the barracks I clambered out of the ditch. Before the entrance there stood a few barrels, placed there as conveniences for the prisoners at night. Suddenly, with a single leap, I landed near one of them and hid there. I did not have to wait long before it was opened from the inside. I pretended that I had just come out of that barrack; then I went in. Here, too, the overcrowding was as suffocating as it had been in No. 17. I had to find room for myself somewhere. I stumbled over human bodies – they struck out at me – I kicked back. It did not matter: nothing mattered any longer. I had to find room – just a little room to sit down.

"Go to hell!" someone growled. "What do you want here?" He kicked me so hard that my stomach turned: the tea adulterated with bromide, the single slice of bread, the half-ounce of margarine, the greenish concoction of soup rose in my gullet....

"You disgusting, filthy swine, vomiting into our faces!"

I realized then that the only way to find some room and save my life was to pit force against force. And when, a few seconds later, I had recovered my wits, I kicked, smashed, and bit until I had obtained a bare foothold for myself in the darkness. At last I was able to sit down. But, though I was overwhelmed by exhaustion, I was unable to sleep. My mind was in a whirl as I thought of all that had happened, and I could not rest in the dreadful congestion, amid people tearing at each other's throats.

When the light of dawn began to trickle into the barrack I glanced around to get my bearings. My neighbor seemed familiar. For a long time I stared dully at his pale face, puzzling at the way his eyebrows met in the middle. Gradually I placed him. It was Uncle Bert, our family doctor all through my childhood years – and now in this twilit dawn, amid death and terror and far from the old life, still the same old "Uncle Bert" to me. This creature lying on the ground in his striped prison clothes had once shone his tiny torch into my throat on a winter evening. It was as he did so that I noticed his eyebrows met in the middle, which made a great impression on my childish mind. Neither I nor Mother, Father, nor even my sister could boast of such a thing. Now, as he lay there on the floor of the crowded barrack, I bent over him and had another look at those eyebrows which, on that long-past feverish winter evening, had made such an indelible imprint on my mind.

He used to be a rich man. A bit haughty, too, with a tendency to talk down to poor people who consulted him. It was difficult to tell whether he was serious or merely joking when he growled: "Look, my boy, your boots are covered with mud, why don't you scrape them clean before you come in here?" And then the poor peasant would go back to the waiting-room to wipe his muddy feet. It paid them to win the favor of such an influential gentleman, for as chief medical officer of the municipality a great deal depended on him: free beds in the hospital, free medicine and the rest. He continued to be looked up to as a "gentleman" even when the dark clouds were gathering in the sky for the rest of his race. The "pillars of society" of the town remained friendly with Bert because – "Well, this Jew makes his money in an honest way." Even when the Jews were herded into the ghetto, his social position remained the same: he became the physician of the ghetto. But by that time the Gentiles were no longer keen to be his friends.

After the German invasion, but still before the ghetto was set up, I had occasion to look up Uncle Bert in connection with my father's case when, after his arrest, he was temporarily imprisoned in the municipal jail. I went to see him to obtain a certificate concerning the heart disease from which my father had actually suffered. He was sitting with his family in his roof garden. They had just finished supper. The gramophone was playing; subdued lights created a pleasant atmosphere; like glow-worms, cigars studded the semi-darkness. Husband and wife were cracking jokes, oblivious of the fact that elsewhere in the town the Germans were plotting a devastation unequalled in history, among whose victims they themselves were destined to be.

"Unfortunately, there's nothing I can do for your dear father. I'm afraid – how shall I put it? – Your father did involve himself …er … in certain Socialist connections with which I have no sympathy. I am sorry for your father because …er … I have always had a great personal regard for him. But a, what's-it-called, a certificate – that, I'm afraid, I cannot give you.…"

I tried to appeal to his heart. I recalled the years of my childhood when he used to be a daily caller at our house. I spoke of the affectionate help which my father had given him in legal matters. I told him that while my father was still in a Hungarian jail, with the help of such a certificate we might be able to get him into a prison hospital. I begged, I entreated – all in vain.

Dazed, in impotent rage, I descended the stairs. Long after I had stepped out into the street the slow rhythm of the gramophone was still throbbing in my ears.

Now he lay there, Uncle Bert, thin as a skeleton, in the midst of the whining, shouting, fighting multitude of the barrack. Gone were his home, his house with the roof garden, his "gentlemanly" attitude, his condescending manner; he lay helpless next to me. Slowly, he opened his eyes. He did not recognize me as, in a whimpering voice, he begged for some warm tea. Outside the barrack in the dawn light they were already beginning to dish out the drugged brew called tea. I went out and brought back a mugful of the steaming liquid. Some fever must have been burning within him; he drank with savage avidity. I felt that I really ought to have hated this man, if it had not been too much of an effort even to hate. But when, having drained the drink to the last drop, the former Medical Officer of Health looked up at me with childish gratitude shining from his eyes, I realized how hard it was to hate if one looked at the world through the eyes of childhood.

# CHAPTER IV

My flight from Barrack No. 17 might have had grave consequences, but there seemed to be little likelihood that the addition of my person to my new barrack would be discovered. During the *Appel* the SS man burst into a roar of abuse when he found there was one more miserable bastard than there should be in Barrack No. 11 (my new home). Swearing, he called on the odd man out to fall out immediately. But the odd man out had had sufficient sense to wash himself in the dirty water earlier in the morning, and was now quite indistinguishable from the others. Still swearing and threatening, the SS man at last added the extra one to the total and marched off.

My new *Blockältester* was a gipsy. He lived in the front part of the barrack in a special room. His two daughters lived on the other side, also in a room partitioned off with boards. When, at the next distribution of our rations, my turn came, one of these gipsy girls handed me my portion – an ounce or so of sausages floating in water, a speck of margarine and a slice of bread. Our eyes met. It seemed an eternity since I had last seen a woman – not that in my tormented state I had desired one. Now the gipsy girl noticed that I was looking at her, she stared back at me with provocative insolence, then burst out laughing. Her laughter was rough and harsh, in strange contrast to her young features. She must have been about seventeen. A red ribbon adorned her thick hair, black as midnight: her toenails were varnished and her mouth was thickly smeared with lipstick.

But the crowd had already swept me on, and a few seconds later I was back inside the barrack, her rough laughter ringing in my ears. Apathetically I sat down on the floor. Next to me the prisoners were talking about the *Blockältester*: how he stole the bulk of our rations and hoarded it in his room.

"We ought to work out a plan to break into his room at night and get back what he's robbed us of," said one, licking his sausage skin.

Another man who was sitting farther away put the lump of margarine in his mouth, swallowed it down and replied:

"You're a fool – don't you know what would happen then? The next morning they'd do us in for good."

But the first one held his own. "Why should they? After all, it is disgusting that the decent rations provided by the SS should be stolen by these swine."

The other became enraged. "O you ape, you big imbecile! Do you think the SS don't know all about it? Do you imagine, you blockhead, that they would dare to steal if the SS didn't encourage them? Don't you realize their methods, you fool, you? Well, let me tell you: first of all the SS storekeepers take their share. Then the mob in the kitchen. After them, it is the turn of those who carry the provisions from the kitchen to the *Blockältester*'s room. Only then, at the tail end, does the Ältester steal his share. And then you squeal about 'decent rations.' Decent, are they? When the bread ration starts off from the stores, it isn't quite half a pound. And by the time it reaches your filthy paws, it is less than one ounce." He spat disdainfully.

"But those who can lick, they do lick up the Ältester's room – they don't have to go short of anything." He pointed enviously to the cleaners standing in front of the *Blockältester*'s room, who were licking the inside of some empty tins.

"Not surprised, are you?" asked my neighbor. "They come from the Felvidek: they're a rubbishy lot."

The other one retorted: "It's you who are the rubbish, you filth, you vomit! It is your sort who create anti-Semitism – you rotten collaborator!"

I moved away from them. I had known both of them in my home town. One had been a high school teacher, the other an electrical engineer.

The barrack now appeared like a market-place gone mad. Wild-eyed, some of the prisoners were attempting to exchange their portion of margarine for bread. Others were bartering margarine for sausage, and others still were throwing their food over the electrified fence and catching the cigarettes thrown in exchange. Some were writhing on the floor with stomach cramps. Some could not move any longer: people just trod on them.

Then someone stopped in front of me; I caught a glimpse of a smooth knee in the shadow, of a gaily colored skirt. The *Blockältester*'s daughter was standing before me. I stood up.

"Do you want to work?" she asked. "You'll get bread."

I nodded silently.

"Well then, get a move on. Follow me!" she said, her voice harsh as before.

She led me to the *Blockältester*'s room. It was a simple room. Two wooden bunks stood by the wall, with uncovered pillows and blankets thrown over them. By a rough trestle table sat the *Blockältester*, a newspaper in his hand, a cigarette dangling from the corner of his mouth. The wall was adorned with the picture of a half-naked female, cut out of some German magazine; next to it hung an image of the Virgin Mary with the infant Jesus. I could not imagine how the cigarette, the pictures, the

42

newspaper and the rest had found their way behind the
bars of Auschwitz. The gipsy looked me up and down.

"If you steal, you'll end up like your predecessor," he
began threateningly, his eyes flashing. "You'll clean the
rooms, fetch water and polish our shoes. That's all. If you
talk too much or steal, you can say goodbye to life. You
can sleep on the threshold or wherever you can find room.
Off you go." And he pushed me out through the door.

As soon as I was outside, the gipsy girl asked me:

"Tell me, can you dance?"

"Dance?" I thought I must have misunderstood her.

"Yes, dance. What's so odd about that question?"

"Oh, of course, of course I can dance," I stammered in
confusion. "Indeed, I can...."

"Well, come along then." We went across to the gipsy
girl's room. It had no window; light oozed in through
holes bored in the boards. An oppressive, sour smell hung
in the air. Cara – that was the girl's name – lit a candle.
By the light of the flickering candle I could see that,
except for the rough wooden bed, the room was quite
empty. A battered old gramophone was standing on the
ground. She wound it up and put on a record, and through
that barracks of Auschwitz trickled the slow melody of
"J'attendrai." In the meantime Cara had brought some
bread, margarine, and jam. I stuffed myself with the food;
the effort of eating covered my forehead with sweat, my
whole body was perspiring. When I could eat no more, I
pushed the tins away from me. Then Cara wanted to
dance. "Teach me to dance the way people used to dance
back home." I could hear shouts and the noise of fighting
from the barrack as we started to dance to the slow
rhythm. I was tired, each step cost me an effort; I longed
to lie down there in that room and sleep, sleep, sleep....
But Cara forced me on. In my striped prison clothes and
shapeless wooden shoes I danced and went on dancing –

"the way we used to dance back home." My stomach was turning – but I had to keep on dancing. I saw before me the familiar dance hall at home, little Eva, the other girls. And behind the music, as I danced on and on, people groaned and screamed, dogs barked in the distance, evil smells afflicted my nostrils. Out of step, out of time, I trudged round in the grip of her sweating, relentless arms.

Then she dragged me to the bed, tore off my jacket and pulled me towards her. My brain was dulled, my body inert, my muscles weary. "Come, make love to me," she breathed into my face. Disgusted, I turned away from her, but she would not let me alone....

In the days following, my conscience carried on a ceaseless dialogue, almost as if two different people were struggling within me. "No, I cannot live in a separate world of my own, while men are perishing next to me by the thousand. I cannot wallow in pleasure while my companions are being destroyed around me."

"And if you give it up?"

"Then I might as well give up life itself."

"But you did not choose this privileged position for yourself. Fate picked on you. If you say 'No' to destiny, you say 'No' to your life, too."

"But I am living on goods robbed from other people. At home I used to fight against this very thing which led up to Auschwitz. How often I used to say that nothing could happen which would shatter my convictions. And now that the time has come to prove myself, I become this whore's pimp."

"Words, mere words, moral inhibitions, products of social conditioning. But have it your own way: stick to your principles. Refuse her – and tomorrow, or the day after, you'll be trembling again with bestial hunger, you'll grow weak and your fellow-men will throw you into the ditch by the electrified fence – because people are bad."

"It isn't true; people aren't bad. They are simply human beings, just like yourself. All they want is to live. They want bread. They want to stretch their legs out at night. They want to lie down with their women. No, people aren't bad; it is the world that's evil...."

There was no end to these inward struggles. And all the time the enormous chimneys of the crematoria spewed forth their smoke by day and fire by night.

One night I was sitting with Cara in front of the barrack. Her naked breasts were illuminated by the fire from the chimneys. Far away dogs were howling; something rumbled with the noise of a distant waterfall. As the flames rose higher and higher above our heads, the stars grew fainter. As we sat there, a night from the distant past strayed into my remembrance, a night back home when I had sat at the edge of a little grove and gazed down into the valley where my native town was sleeping peacefully. It was all infinitely far away.

"What are you staring at?" she asked abruptly.

"I am looking at the fire."

"What's there to look at in that? They aren't burning *us*."

How alien this girl was to me, with her wretched body in which the soul had never had a chance to come to human fruition. She must have been a mere child when they dragged her away from the Berlin suburb where she used to live and the first Gestapo soldier lowered himself on to her brown-skinned body. She knew nothing of the world which lay beyond the mountains, beyond the muddy waste that surrounded the camp. She did not know that beyond the fire of the crematoria there were cities in which neon lights were glittering at the moment, and countries where the city lights no longer burned but where the night was filled with the wailing of sirens, and flames which enveloped homes, buildings, memories, everything.

No, one could not tell Cara that not so far away, there lived poets who wrote verses, artists who created music and painted pictures. Cara would not have understood such a world. It was here that she had first sat in a car – an SS car. It was here that she had first listened to a radio, in the SS kitchen. Sometimes when she was silent her features softened into an expression of calm and tenderness. But no sooner did she open her mouth than her face turned hard and crude and she became a member of Auschwitz, just like the rest of us.

SS soldiers with weapons at the ready and the emblem of skull and crossbones in their caps guarded us on each side of the camp; from the watchtowers machineguns were kept trained on us.

In a sentry box by the enormous iron gate that led from the gipsy encampment to the other part of the camp an SS soldier was posted to look after the electric switches which controlled the supply of electricity in the fences. Beyond the barbed wire fence of the gipsy camp, farther away, yet more fences were erected, so that if someone had ever managed to escape across the first hurdle, he would still have had to overcome a second, a third and even a fourth obstacle. Outside the gipsy camp the road was uneven and muddy. Huge, whitewashed pits disfigured the site, surrounded by scattered heaps of sand; wooden beams were strewn about the place. They must have started to build something here, then changed their minds. Further off a small wood was discernible, and beyond it the lifeless sky. Apart from the bloodhounds, kept to guard us, there was no sign of any living creature. Under the damp bricks sunk into the ground no soft-bellied insects crawled. Even birds did not fly over the barbed wire fence of Auschwitz. It was a cold, dead world.

The weather was sad and gloomy; it started to drizzle, and our thin clothes were quickly wet through. We had been taken to work in the women's camp. On the previous evening Cara had mentioned that I would be detailed there, and she had instructed me to purchase some lipstick from one of the female *Blockältesters* with a box of sardines. The SS men left us at the entrance to the women's camp, and from there we continued our journey under specially appointed prisoners, *Kapos* (prisoner functionaries) and some *Vorarbeiter* (foremen). The Polish Kapo who was in charge of our lot knew all about Cara's commission, and when we stopped he signaled to me to go to the barrack I had been told about. But in my excitement (would I perhaps meet some of my old acquaintances there?) I mistook the number of the barrack and entered the wrong one. It was completely empty. I was about to walk out when my Kapo appeared in the doorway accompanied by a thin, pallid woman with a bald, shaven head. In my fright I crawled under one of the bunks, fearing that the Kapo might beat me to death if he saw that I had come to the wrong barrack. He was busy haggling with the woman. At first I did not understand what it was all about, but before long the horrible truth dawned in my mind.

"A third of a loaf will do, won't it?" The Kapo asked.

"Please, make it a half," the woman implored him. The Kapo responded with a savage blow at the miserable creature's bosom.

"Either you lie down with me for the third of a loaf, or else you lie down without any bread at all!" He threw the woman roughly on to the bunk. She cried out with pain.

"Shut up – stop screaming!" the Kapo silenced her. "Come on to the top bunk. Nobody will see us there." He produced a chunk of bread and gave it to the woman. While they were climbing up on to the bunk, the woman began to gnaw the bread. She seemed a worn-out, sickly creature, something halfway between a human being and a beast. A kerchief was loosely tied around her head; the long dress she wore must once have been an evening dress. Through her torn rags wounds were visible on her body. She must have been on *Schonung* (forbearance), that is, a day's sick-leave from work. Disease was written all over her as she clambered up on to the top bunk to yield her desiccated body to the Kapo. Trembling, I watched them from my hide-out, watched the Kapo working himself up to a pitch of frenzy, I heard his fists pounding at the sick woman in sadistic ecstasy until, with a last smack, he signaled that the act was over. The wan wretch of a woman staggered off the bunk and passed close by me. It was as if a dagger had stabbed me to the heart as in that distorted, haggard face I recognized one of my sister's friends. Once she had been a beautiful, happy young girl.

Marta had come to our town from the capital after her father had been appointed local branch manager of a big, nationwide bedding and soft furnishing company. Her parents were converted to Roman Catholicism as soon as the discriminative laws against Jews began to be applied. They imagined that, if they adopted Roman Catholicism, the Catholic Church would stand by them if any trouble threatened. But they made the fundamental mistake of most proselytes at that time: they tried to adopt all the inherent opinions and characteristics of dyed-in-the-wool Christians, including anti-Semitism. When they arrived in our town, Marta's parents avoided all Jewish society like the plague, declaring that they "did not feel happy among Israelites." But the distance between Budapest and our town being only 150 miles, just far enough for everybody to know everything about everyone else, it soon became known that the local branch manager of the great bedding and soft furnishing company was by no means the true-blue Christian he made out – and the gentlefolk of the neighborhood remained aloof. Occasionally one of the young dandies tried to flirt with Marta, but she had no time for such empty-headed fellows: she had found her proper social level long before her parents did.

Once Marta made a big scene at home.

"Can't you see that they won't accept us as one of them? If they run after me, it's only because they think I'm easy meat."

Her mother cast a pained glance at her husband as she replied: "If your soul is heavy, go to the Confessional, my daughter."

But it was soon made clear to the branch manager and his wife that Marta was right: that whether they admitted it or not, whether they liked it or not, they were not counted as Christians. And by then the Jews themselves would have nothing to do with them.

My sister and Marta had become friends after being in the same class at school, and it was in our house that Marta made the acquaintance of a schoolmaster who had an even greater guilt on his conscience than his religion: he professed to be a Socialist. The two young people fell deeply in love, and before long the schoolmaster proposed to Marta.

"My own daughter marry a teacher, a ... Jew, a Socialist? Never, never!" her father bellowed, quite beside himself with rage.

Her mother merely sighed as she said: "Is this how you show your gratitude to us, my little girl? How can you insist on marrying beneath your station?"

"What exactly *is* our station?" Marta asked.

"We're distinguished business people," her mother replied. "And you have a handsome dowry, too."

49

That same evening Marta left her parents' house and spent the night with us. Next day she married the schoolmaster and the same day her parents made a formal announcement to the employees and customers in the shop:

"We have disowned our daughter. We no longer know her."

Marta and her husband lived together very happily for a time. But the Nazi menace was catching up with the schoolmaster, and he was arrested and interned. About the same time Marta's father received a telegram from the capital, requesting him to report immediately at the head office. As soon as he arrived he was shown in to the managing director.

"My dear friend, um, um ... I am in a most awkward position. I fear it is my unpleasant task to inform you that the board has decided to dispense with your services."

The old man was stunned. "But, Sir, why? What have I done?"

"Well, my dear friend, well ... um, um ... you realize you are a thingamajig, how shall I put it ..."

"But I am not a thingamajig," protested the old man. "I am a Christian."

The managing director lost his patience. "Let us not play with words. You know very well that you are merely a converted Jew."

Completely crushed, the old man returned home, yet the calamity which forced him to leave the business which he valued even more highly than his own daughter could not shatter his pride. But the mother broke down. Secretly, unknown to her husband, she tried to contact Marta. She approached my father.

"I know that you must despise me. I'm a despicable creature. I have committed the worst crime a parent can commit – I have disowned my child." She began to sob.

"I dare not tell my husband but I can tell you this. Although I have been baptized into the Catholic Church I pray now from the prayer book which my dear mother once gave me. The Lord God has punished me. O how cruelly He has visited me." She tried hard to control her tears.

"You also are a father, and I know that you're fond of my daughter. Please talk to her. Try to persuade her to make it up with us – at least with me, her mother."

At first my father wanted to refuse the woman's request, as he told us afterwards. He did not wish to interfere in a family quarrel. But he felt so sorry for her that next day he spoke to Marta.

"Your mother came to see me yesterday. She has learnt to regret deeply the way she treated you. My advice to you would be not to bear a grudge against her."

"Do you know, Uncle, that I am soon to have a child myself?" replied Marta, weeping. "How could I bear a grudge against my mother!"

So a secret meeting was arranged between mother and daughter, without the father's knowledge. They fell into each other's arms as if they had just returned from some long journey.

It was about this time that the Germans invaded the country and the ghettos were set up. In the face of this threat Marta's father had converted all his money into jewelry and buried it in the ground near a well. He did not tell even his wife where it was hidden. Strangers were now giving the orders in his former shop; other people lived in his house. Having denied the God whom his parents had taught him to revere in his childhood, he could find no solace in his newly acquired religion. The ground seemed to have slipped from under his feet. He belonged nowhere. And on top of it all he had lost his daughter whom he had loved so dearly.

Every evening, driven by irrepressible uneasiness, he paced the winding and twisting streets in the small area of the ghetto. When Marta gave birth to a son in a small house in the ghetto he could not pretend that he had not heard the news. His wife wrung her hands as she begged him to go and see his little grandchild.

"I don't know who you are talking about. The person you speak of is dead as far as I'm concerned," he answered.

Then came the rumor that the ghetto was to be evacuated and all its inhabitants deported. A few days before the evacuation of the ghetto some "counter-espionage investigators" arrived from the capital city. Their "counter-espionage" activity consisted in setting up a form of devilish inquisition in order to find out where the ghetto-dwellers had hidden their money and valuables. One day the old man was told to report, together with his wife – and Marta, too.

For the first time in several years the whole family met together again. The young woman was only just over her confinement: she came to the inquisition weak and exhausted. But the policeman on duty would not allow her to sit down.

"Once you're in there, you'll have a chance to lie down, young lady," he said, pointing towards the next room from which issued demented cries. Then the three of them were pushed into the room of "investigation." One of the "investigators" immediately pounced upon the old woman. He tore off her dress and began to beat her wrinkled breasts with a truncheon. Terrified, her husband entreated them: "Gentlemen, in the name of Christ ... Don't ... Don't ..." Another one jumped at Marta and stripped her naked. She gave a piercing shriek.

"Let me alone – I've just had a baby! I am a mother!" Like wild beasts they dug their knees into her abdomen, and her father saw a flood of blood gush from his daughter's body. As for his wife, they connected an electrical apparatus to her teats and loins, which spasmodically shook the emaciated old woman with infernal ferocity. Then one of the thugs stepped up to the old man and struck him across the face with his truncheon.

"Well, Jew, are you going to tell us where you hid the stuff? Are you going to tell us now, you Jew?" The broken set of false teeth dropped out of the old man's mouth. He heard his daughter's screams and the groans of his wife; and he answered in a toothless whisper:

"I'll tell you, for God's sake, I'll tell you." And he told them in exact detail where he had concealed the wealth for which he had toiled a lifetime, forsaken his forefathers' God and disowned his daughter.

Then, with bleeding bodies, they were thrust out to lie under the blazing summer sun in the factory yard where the Gestapo had driven the people from the ghetto in order to facilitate the "smooth transaction" of their business. At sunset that day Marta's mother died. And when Uncle Bert had officially confirmed her death, the old man turned to face the East. Swaying on his feet, he uttered the ancient prayer which he had been taught as a child, as he listened to the rabbi addressing the people of the ghetto.

"My brethren, the way from Babylonia to this day is but a step in time, for hate is everywhere the same. This hatred ought to teach us where we belong. We are children of an unfortunate, lost and tortured people. Since we have lost our homeland, we have never known stable ground beneath our feet. We must understand, my brethren, that there is no way out from the predicament in which the Lord of Hosts had seen fit to place us. There is no escape. With batons and bayonets, with their twisted cross and their crooked laws they will herd us together into a single flock." He cast a glance at the dead woman, then went on:

"My brethren, this wretched woman denied us in vain; she sought refuge under the sheltering wings of another faith to no avail. It was among her own people that she breathed her last breath. We cannot bury her in a cemetery. We shall lay her body in a grave by the canal; may it rest there until the Lord God brings about the resurrection of the dead. But we, my brethren, are about to set out on an uncertain journey. Who knows if any one of us will ever return? Yet if any one does return it will be his duty to tell the world – the world which has not been contaminated by the plague of the twisted cross – how human beings have been turned out of their homes to lie helpless in their own blood for want of a single soul to raise a finger in their defense."

That night everyone expected a miracle to happen. But it never came. No milk flowed from Marta's crushed breasts for her baby – and next day it was over his grandchild that the old man pronounced the prayer for the dead. So did the dawn arrive which saw us crammed into the trucks and dragged away – to Auschwitz.

"Marta, Marta!" I cried as I recognized her. She took a few steps towards me. For a moment her eyes seemed to light up with recognition: then it passed, and a pair of eyes clouded with lunacy was peering into mine.

"I'm hungry … I want to eat … give me some bread and I'll lie down with you."

Horrified, I ran out of the barrack.

# CHAPTER V

Until I met Marta that day in the barrack I had begun to forget that once emotion had vibrated like a melody within me, that I could be one in spirit with the lives of others, share in the unfolding of their joys and sorrows. But now this encounter brought down an avalanche of memories upon me, and the past was brought back into sharp relief. As I closed my eyes that night I distinctly heard the voices of old acquaintances walking along the streets where I had so often met them – haughty ones who hardly acknowledged one's greeting and modest ones who would hail one first. Each with their familiar mannerisms, they came to meet me in the feverish night and then disappeared down the old street which, by now, might well have been destroyed by bombs. Calmly they filed past as they had done before the war, and then they turned to face me once more, dark and distorted, their eyes sunk deep into their sockets – a terrifying apparition.

Many times in the night I started up, only to fall back again into this nightmare state. I was perched on a ledge which overlooked the dizzy chasm of insanity, down in whose depths my memories were revolving like so many hungry whirlpools, threatening to suck me down and down.

But the routine of camp life continued. For hours on end we stood during the morning roll call and evening roll call. Fewer and fewer of the old crowd were left, and the chimneys of the crematoria threw up their flames by night as if it were part of a firework display. Only in the gypsies' quarter did everything remain the same.

I spent every evening with Cara. By now I felt she was the only creature to whom I could talk and who could understand me. Was it love that developed between us during those slowly moving days? I do not know. If it was love, it was an Auschwitz brand of love. It was a mixture of numbness, suffering, hopelessness, death and the writhing agony of pleasure. I was little different from Cara now. Poetry, music and painting did not enter my thoughts any more. I, like the others, was only preoccupied with scheming how to grab a bigger chunk of bread, with rejoicing that it was not we who were being burnt that night. My brutality, my violence, the extinction of my moral sense not longer worried me. As if knocked on the head, my conscience lay unconscious somewhere in the deep recesses of my soul, no longer able to remind me of the eternal laws of humanity. The sight of people lying in their congealed blood in the ditch beneath the electrified fence had ceased to quicken my pulse. My fists were no longer itching to get at the murderers. I was a man of Auschwitz. Only rarely, and only while dreaming, could I weep – and when I woke up I did not know why I had been crying.

I roamed aimlessly among the gipsy barracks. I saw their days and their nights, their embraces and the grunting expression of their delights. I recognized that their standard of living was a great deal better than our own, but I no longer asked myself why they deserved a more privileged lot. Nothing could make me wonder any more.

Not until a new horror took place one night. Everything happened as if in a nightmare. Afterwards I could only remember being blinded by the headlamps that shone into my eyes out of the darkness of the night, and hearing a sudden commotion and screaming from the gipsy quarter as the SS lorries carried the gypsies out of the camp. And then I no longer felt Cara's body beside me.

I do not know how long it took them to liquidate the gypsies. But when at dawn I noticed the scattered pots, the torn garments before the empty barracks, at last I realized that I would never see Cara again. The fate of Auschwitz had overtaken the gypsies, too. I burst into tears. For hours I wept hysterically, as if all the tragedy I had previously experienced, all the terror of days, weeks and months, had overwhelmed me in that one night. And in Cara's destruction I sensed my own.

A few days later, following a last sorting-out, we were herded into trucks again. We did not know until the very moment the train pulled out whether we were bound for the gas chambers or not. Then through the small, iron-grilled window I saw the barracks of Auschwitz becoming smaller and smaller in the distance: the smoke looming above the camp grew fainter also and at last merged into the grey sky. I dropped inert into a corner of the truck. "I have survived Auschwitz – but what now?"

As I turned towards the wall of the truck, my hand hit something hard. It was a small album of photographs, left there probably by some other deportee, someone who might have arrived that day, or the day before, on the same train, from anywhere in Europe. A special squad was usually assigned to the task of emptying the trucks. Probably in their haste they had not noticed the small album.

I opened it. A woman in an out-moded dress stared at me from the first page. It was one of those typical photographs taken about the beginning of this century. The legend underneath the picture was merely: "Mother, 1906." On the next page a young girl was laughing into my eyes. She was sitting on the concrete edge of a swimming pool, her hair streaming with water. I could almost visualize her in front of me: how they threw her into the water, how she fell in with a little scream, how she climbed gaily out....

And now she was sitting there at the side of the pool, unaware that someone to whom she must have been dear had clicked the camera.

Another picture. A young lad's eyes smiled into the dimness of the truck. Underneath was written: "To Mommy, from her loving Buksi." There on the next page was the girl again, standing serenely in her bridal dress, a middle-aged man next to her. Another photograph – a big party in a garden. There they all are: mother, aunts, husband and wife. How sad this woman looks! What could have happened to her? A small bungalow. An elderly lady is leaning out of the window, and the outlines of a cat are visible through the curtain. And here is an old picture – isn't it funny? – Karoly the Fourth, last king of the monarchy, shaking hands with some soldiers standing in front of him. Well, now, if that isn't the husband! In the uniform of a captain, what a happy smile on his face! Then two snapshots: Quarnero, Italy, 1934. A young woman and a suntanned man are looking towards the lens. Hey, that one is Buksi again – how on earth did they get to Italy? Then Buksi in various poses: in the garden, picking some fruit off a tree, very conscious of being photographed, turning his head somewhat artificially towards the camera. Buksi in his study: judging by the instruments scattered on the drawing board, Buksi must be an engineer. Another picture: to Dr. and Mrs. Ignac Szagola, very sincerely, Henrik Haber, art photographer. Probably an extra copy, ordered from the photographer. A woman lying in a clean, white bed, holding a small baby in her arms, beside her the husband, his face radiant – no Buksi anywhere – underneath, the words: "Csopi, born on September 7, 1942." More pictures, pictures, pictures ...

the past coming to life, a family coming to life. People who had been strangers to me suddenly became acquaintances. An old lady, a young girl, Buksi, the husband, Dr. Szagola, where are you now, all of you? Where is that small baby, where the unknown woman leaning out of the window? Where is the sun that shone through the cracks of the shutters – where did the past vanish?

The truck was very quiet. People were lying about in a stupor as the train raced along. We were being carried to slave labor – somewhere.

As night fell the memories crept back again: they came, one after the other, in a weary, heavy-footed row. And the wheels of the carriage kept hammering out the rhythm: Hungary ... Hungary ... Hungary. ... Sleep seemed reluctant to close my eyes. Shreds of talk from right and left drifted towards me in the dark truck.

"And then I told my wife," somebody was saying, "look dear, these shoes will be far too big for you. But she insisted on buying them. And then she complained that the shoes were too big...."

People spoke about the past. Some tried to sleep.

Two SS soldiers were sitting in the middle of the truck, their weapons at the ready. One kept his eye on the left half of the truck; the other covered the right-hand half. Hungary ... Hungary ... Hungary ... the rails reverberated. Like some tune which gets tangled up in one's mind and cannot be driven out, so did the name of my country whirl round my dizzy brain. And suddenly I saw before me my nursery room – the nursery with the little bed in which I used to sleep every night. I saw before me the flames of the open stove, lighting up the ceiling, casting moving shadows on the walls which, like so many fearsome devils, now stretched out, now withdrew their claws. Beyond the window was the night, and snow was falling in large, white flakes. I saw myself in the white featherbed. At times the fire crackled in a strange tongue. Someone turned on the tap in the kitchen.

"What use will it be if the Allies do win in the end?" I heard someone's voice coming from the depths of the reverberating truck. "By then we shall all be dead."

Hungary … Hungary … Hungary … the rails rattled beneath us.

The bed sat in the corner of the room like a little yellow prison. It was made of brass. When they put me to bed, they pulled up the wooden bars and fixed them with string, so that I should not fall out.

"Little Jancsi must go to sleep," Mother said. "All little boys ought to be asleep by now."

"But I am not a little boy," I whimpered.

When Mother had left me alone, silence prevailed. Then out of the silence came the voices: the voices of the fire, the voice of the wind, the voice of the water tap, and last of all, the voice of silence itself – a strange, chirping, hissing, buzzing sound which I greatly feared. Terrified, I lifted my head out of the featherbed.

All of a sudden the screaming of air raid sirens from the depths of the present night brought me to my senses. Like wounded beasts they wailed. Then silence returned, and once more the past unfolded.

The carpet reached as far as the wardrobe: squares linked up with other squares in its pattern, like a number of trapped, wriggling crosses, or the slithering of snakes. A silvery key kept a melancholy vigil in the lock of the wardrobe, within which dwelt a world of whiteness – Daddy's shirts, Mommy's clothes, tablecloths and bedspreads. Hidden somewhere here was that many-layered black wallet with all sorts of leaflets and cards which Mother used to collect over the years tucked into it: I was allowed to play with them when I was ill. Here also was the small mahogany music box. When it was wound up for me, I could watch the little disc revolving behind the glass and listen to the tinkling music.

Next to the wardrobe was the window, a double window. In summer flies crawled between the panes, seeking a way to the open air. And then there was the mirror, with its two folding wings. At a certain angle they would reflect a whole infinity of Me's. I played with it often. When they put me to bed I used to think of the innumerable little boys left inside the mirror – were they, too, put to bed by their mother? Next to the mirror came the bed, my parents' bed. In the mornings I frequently paid a visit to this bed. It was so wonderfully warm there, under Mommy's blanket....

"Little Jancsi must sleep now," I heard my Mother's voice from the distance. "Little boys should be asleep by now."

How clearly and sharply I saw myself, such a brief while ago, on this dreadful night! I was afraid not so much of the forces of the external world as of the powers of the universe within, the odd, mysterious universe of childhood, until, with bombs exploding in the distance, I became momentarily more aware of the peril which was now threatening from without. Then, for a long time, no images came at all. I just sat in the dark, my head bent over my knees. But later the darkness began to loosen up again, and in the slowly pulsing twilight of this darkness fresh pictures arrived.

The park in the suburb, set beneath the cloister on the hillside. Here stood the pavilion, a restaurant built of logs where on Sundays the stolid citizens, perched on benches, listened to the band. The wind was blowing from the direction of the river; Mother, sitting on a bench, was knitting a pullover. Further away some pensioners were sitting, savoring their pipes with slow puffs beneath their big mustaches. By the fountain a few children were playing. As the sun began to set, the rust-colored rays lit up Mother's hair. "How lovely you look, Mommy!" I said, and she smiled. In a little while, when the wind grew stronger and brought the chill of the north with it, we set out for home along the tree-lined road.

"Do you see those trees bending, Jancsi?" she asked. "Do you know what makes them move?"

"The wind," I answered proudly.

"Would you like to play the wind-game?"

The long road was quite deserted; hand in hand we started walking. The slow steps counted as a "breeze," we went faster when Mother said "wind," and then we ran as she shouted "storm." And then she picked me up high in the air, running as she held me. "Whirlwind, whirlwind," she whispered, exhausted by the effort. We reached the street. The bell of the near-by church rang its summons. A man riding a bicycle, holding a long pole, triggered the dim flames of the gas lamps into brightness under the evening sky ... and ... and I was thinking that one day I would grow up and not have Mother by my side any more....

"Hungary ... Hungary ... Hungary ..." the wheels of the truck wailed on. Large tears rolled down my cheeks. "I did grow up, Mommy, I did grow up...."

I was deathly tired by then. But my tormenting memories gave me no rest, as I looked back at the fearful pattern that had brought me to this time and place.

March 11, 1938 – the Germans had occupied Austria. The news swept over our town like a great flood that Saturday morning. Then, slowly, the flood sank back to the cold river bed; but the mud and the drifting rubbish it had brought with it stayed behind. The Nazi press had tasted blood. Now the walls of Hungarian buildings were covered with signs of the arrow-crossed and provocative posters, and new anti-Jewish words were sung to the old tunes.

Then came the demonstrations. With feathers stuck in their caps, calling themselves "Hungarians," a mob of louts paraded through the streets of our small town yelling their beastly slogans over and over again: "Down with the Jews – down with the Czechs – Benes must go!" The "Nationalists," the so-called "Christians," in the name of the nation, of Hungary and of Christianity set up the assembly-line of hatred in their presses and on their platforms. Articles were featured in the extreme right-wing press, purporting to show how these filthy Jews infiltrated into Hungary from Polish Galicia in order to contaminate the life of honest Christians. Jewry of the whole world was hatching a single, vast, secret plot, aiming directly and exclusively at the annihilation of Christian Hungary. In this conspiracy could be found all Jewish Big Businessmen, Jewish Communists, the rabbis, the students at the Talmudic academies, every rotten, rascally Jew who had cunningly wormed his way into Hungary from abroad. These articles and slogans served as the psychological preparation for the gas chambers and the crematoria. Decent non-Jews who did not lose their human and Christian sense of value were branded as "hirelings of the Jews." Then came the Jewish laws. The first one was entitled "The Act for Social Reconstruction." At this stage the "Christian and Hungarian" gentlemen still observed the forms of polite verbiage. And the Regent, whose greatest success in life had been in managing to make a silk purse out of a sow's ear, was sitting pretty in the Palace in Buda, playing bridge with Jewish and non-Jewish big industrialists and landlords while he cast an occasional affectionate glance at his wife who, according to rumor, was herself of Jewish extraction. The masters of Hungary did not realize that by the enactment of the Jewish Laws they had issued their own death warrant too. When the fire broke out, it did not avoid either them or their houses.

In the newspapers, in the official press, the country's "Christian spirit and morality" was defended against the assaults of the Freuds, the Yehudi Menuhins, the Einsteins, the Stefan Zweigs. And for a long time, for a very long time, the clergy kept silent – the Catholic Church as well as the rest. When, timidly, they did raise their voices, it was already too late.

Yet in that same Parliament in which the elders of the nation (not elected by secret ballot) held their sessions and passed laws at the Government's bidding, there were a few voices which represented true humanity and Christianity. Anna Kethly, for instance, whom the "chivalrous gentlemen" nicknamed "the red rat." How nobly and bravely this frail, Socialist woman fought for the interests of the oppressed, without the use of a single harsh word. But there were few Anna Kethlys. The "open" electoral system meant punishment for all voters who let it be known before the official electoral committee that they would not vote for the government's candidate. In the countryside gendarmes stood with fixed bayonets outside the polling booths, and woe to the peasant who dared to squeal against his masters.

This wretched peasantry, numbering four million persons, had been under the yoke of the landowners for centuries, beaten and driven to labor in the name of "Christianity and Hungary." Their only right was to get dead drunk on Saturdays and occasionally to thrash their wives in desperation. Their masters saw to it that the knowledge of reading or writing did not, God forbid, reach the peasant; or if it did, they took pains to make sure that he had no time, or nerves, or energy to make use of it. Books could have been dangerous weapons in the peasant's hand. One could have cried at the misery, both spiritual and material, of the Hungarian villagers. The peasant kept quiet.

And what of the two million industrial workers, with their unsatisfactory working conditions, long hours of work, and minimum of welfare facilities? A small section of them were, and remained, conscious Social Democrats. But the majority was swallowed up by the whale of Fascism. They thought that if they could take everything away from the Jews they would have all they wanted for themselves, and all their problems would be finally solved.

The middle class, standing over the bleeding body of the working population and the peasantry, were faithful parrots to the "Christian Hungarian Monarchy." They loathed the Jews who "had taken away their bread" – for the Jew, not being a gentleman, worked hard for his livelihood, and at the beginning of the century working for one's living seemed despicable to a Hungarian gentleman. Yet the Jewish Laws hit hard not so much the "big" Jews as the thousands and thousands of small people. The big Jewish industrialist or business man was able to keep his factory or shop going almost up to the German occupation in March, 1944, though as early as 1939 small Jewish clerks were being sacked in order to "restore the correct social balance." Destitution and despair became the lot of these small people. Later on – still before the deportations – they were drafted into labor brigades. First they were deprived of their soldier's uniform; then they were distinguished by red-white-green ribbons (the Hungarian national colors) tied on their left arms; then, a few months later, their ribbon of identification was replaced by a yellow one – and they were free to breathe their last on the minefields of

Ukraine, whither the chivalrous Christian-Hungarian officers had driven them.

Admiral Horthy, Regent of Hungary, had indeed made his silken purse – a type of fascism which managed to maintain a feudal order; Jewish laws which liquidated the small Jews only. Just to accentuate the inherent contradictions of the regime, in the middle of the war one could still read in Hungary the works of Karl Marx, the Hungarian translation of the Beveridge Plan, and many other books by well-known British, American and Russian authors. While the right-wing press was raving and ranting against the Jews, the left-wing papers caricatured and attacked the Nazis. The official organ of the Social Democrats described the world after the war, assuming beyond a doubt that the Allies would be the victors. In Parliament, after the tiny country of Hungary had declared war on Britain and the Soviet Union, one member still dared to declare: "This war is not our war; our allies are really our enemies; our enemies are in truth our allies." In fact, the gentlemen in power were not quite sure who would win in the end, so they tried to play safe and have it both ways. That is why there was perhaps more freedom during the war years in Hungary than before.

And while the countryside was poor and sad, a dark and desolate reminder of the Middle Ages, Budapest, the capital city, continued to glitter. A neutral traveler from abroad would have felt perfectly at home in this city of a million people, the only Hungarian city of European standards. The traffic, the theaters, the cinemas, the night clubs with their English diseuses, the bubbling champagne and the gipsy music created a false atmosphere of peace. Foreigners imagined that all Hungary was like Budapest. In reality the capital was a tremendous burden on the shoulders of the rest of the country.

Yet the coin had another side, too: Trianon. The peace treaty signed in the Palace of Versailles had crippled Hungary, annexing as it did millions of Hungarians and enormous tracts of land to Czechoslovakia, Rumania and Yugoslavia. This inhuman and unjust peace treaty contributed to the multitude of tragedies in Hungary between the two World Wars, for which responsibility rests not only with Admiral Horthy and his governments, but also with the big powers which forced such an intolerable treaty upon the Hungarian people. Auschwitz and the crematoria were set up not only by those infected by the plague of Nazism but also by the great democracies. For that unutterable suffering which befell mankind, the whole world was responsible.

I grew to manhood in this atmosphere of glaring contradictions. To me Hungary meant not a type of chauvinism, but the warmth of home. Nor did I learn my ideas of Christianity from the notices, framed in the national colors, which hung in many shop windows, declaring them a "Christian Hungarian Business" – I learnt them from the kindly lips of Auntie Gizi, who told me, one evening of summer as the moon and the stars crowned her hair like a sparkling diadem, that Jesus had died on the Cross for me, too, and that Christianity meant more than incitement to hate. I understood what she meant by Christianity when, after the German invasion, she called on us and offered money to my father. (Auntie Gizi and Mother had been old friends.) But when, branded with the yellow star, I fled to the Catholic bishop of my town and its priests, begging them to help a few of us young Jews by letting us work on the bishop's estate where the Germans might let us alone, they did not teach me, the Jew, that love is the greatest power on this earth.

Within a minute I found myself politely ushered out of the bishop's palace. But the gipsy girl who was our maid was overcome by weeping in the empty flat when my father was arrested, and went down on her knees and prayed for us all. I am a Jew; but at that moment I understood that the God to whom we all pray, Jews and Christians, is the selfsame God. I knelt down next to her, and while she sobbed the words of "Our Father," I cried to the high, cold March sky: "Hear, O Israel, our Lord is One!" I owe my faith in people and in Christians to a simple woman, a servant girl. Alas, there were few like them.

I was also Hungarian to the marrow of my bones by reason of the language which had been taught to me by my mother, and in which throughout centuries our great writers and poets had expressed Man, his aims, sufferings and struggles, in wonderful colors. It was the language in which, in hours of despair, I cursed my fate, or else implored the help of Heaven....

...As even now I implored it, from the cattle truck in which I was being taken to slave labor, God knew where. Hungary ... Hungary ... rattled the wheels and the rails. And I prayed.

# CHAPTER VI

The train halted briefly in a station. I was able to read the time on the station clock. Somewhere a bell was ringing and from a distance a voice could be heard calling "Ja, hier Weimar" (Yes, here Weimar). Sirens wailed through the empty streets. I could see a strange procession winding its way around one of the turnings – armed children marching in black uniforms. They must have been about fourteen or fifteen years old. They were singing, a song as chill as the wind howling above the streets. Through the iron grill of the window of the truck I watched this fearful march-past: I could imagine it illustrating a poster, with the legend printed across it in large, gory letters: Weimar, 1944.

Curious eyes peered from the windows of the houses near to the station. I noticed a woman clutching a baby in her arms. When that mother puts that toddler into his playpen, I wondered, will he be surrounded with toy soldiers, leaden Hitlers? Was there a little machine gun in his nursery, just a plaything, with the manufacturer's mark on the back, "Made in Germany"? It only takes about fourteen years for toy weapons to assume dangerous, lethal proportions.

The train jerked on. Laboring away, two locomotives pulled it towards the mountains. Dense forests appeared on either side, and the fresh fragrance of the woods seeped into the truck. Felled trees lay about the ground. Where would this journey end at last? It was two days since we had left Auschwitz; two days since we had last tasted food or water. Were we going to get anything to eat? Should we have a chance to sleep? Suddenly there was the sound of a whistle, and the air vibrated with clipped words of command. The train came to a stop.

I looked around. Huge stone buildings dwarfed the station at which we had arrived. We could see even from a distance that they were military barracks. On a tree by the wayside was a poster which featured a mocking caricature of a Catholic priest, a Jew and a Communist. We were escorted on both sides by SS soldiers, guns ready to shoot. It began to rain. At last we arrived at what looked like the gates of a fortress. A machine gun was trained on us as we passed through to the so-called upper camp. Then, after some more gates, we reached the "quarantine," a camp which consisted only of tents. Before long the head prisoners came out to meet us. They wore a red triangle on their civilian clothes – the sign of political prisoners. One of them spoke:

"You have arrived at Buchenwald. Soon enough you'll learn the difference between Auschwitz and Buchenwald. Comradeship is law number one here. Most of us are political prisoners; on the whole, you are not. But you, too, were compelled to leave your country by the same force which drove us here. All of us are victims of Nazism. That is why we must be united. The SS command did not provide any rations for you tonight. But the Norwegian students, when they heard of your arrival this afternoon, offered to give up their bread rations to you. Our French comrades have offered their portion of margarine for today. The Yugoslav group will be fetching some hot soup before long. Everybody will get his provisions in exactly equal measure; nobody gets less and no one may get more. It is forbidden to swap about with your food rations. What they give us is little enough in any case, and every bit is needed to survive at all. Probably you'll only stay in Buchenwald for a short while, after which you'll be sent out to work at one of the outer camps. But while you are here, and let us hope afterwards, too, you will live according to the laws of Buchenwald."

These were the first humane words that had been addressed to us for a long time, the first act of generosity we had encountered. Not long afterwards we received our provisions; we fell on our food with the intensity of the starved. Then we all dispersed to the tents, and sought our rest in the bunks. There were enough blankets to go round, and we could warm our limbs which had become numb in the freezing rain. Soon people began to talk in the dark. Some, thinking of the head prisoner's friendly words, voiced their anxiety – was it right to talk politics in such a camp where, after all, there were SS soldiers about?

"It had a very red smell, all that that character said a little while ago. Pretty words, but mere words," said one voice in the darkness. The speaker used to be managing director of a factory in the country. Someone answered:

"Of course, now that you've gobbled up all the food of these people you call reds, it's easy enough to start slinging mud at them. A few hours were enough for you to forget Auschwitz, eh?"

"Come off it," said the ex-factory bass, "just because of Auschwitz need we jump to the conclusion that the whole world ought to be painted red?"

"There is only one conclusion you should have jumped to, and that is the answer to who set up Auschwitz."

"Who did? The Germans, of course," replied the managing director. At this, the other retorted:

"I'll tell you who did it: it was the nationalistic capitalists."

"Oh yes, indeed! You people always have a few trite slogans ready at hand, to be dragged forth on any occasion."

"Excuse me," interjected a third one. I was almost overcome by surprise at seeing these men of Auschwitz transformed into reasonably polite beings by means of Norwegian bread, French margarine and Serbian soup. "Excuse me, but you don't seriously think that it was the capitalists who helped Hitler? Such an idea is all the more preposterous since there were many Jews among the capitalists. You cannot really imagine that a Jew would help his own enemies?"

"It is irrelevant to the question what I do or don't imagine," answered the previous speaker harshly. "But one thing is certain. Directly or indirectly, they did pave Hitler's way to power."

I was unable any longer to follow this ever-broadening discussion. Weariness weighed heavy upon me, and I sank into deep sleep.

After two or three weeks at Buchenwald we were again herded into cattle trucks for yet one more journey. This time, however, the journey lasted less than a day. The village where we arrived was called Tröglitz. As we alighted from the trucks I wondered whether I would ever again in my life sit in an ordinary passenger compartment, or whether my predestined lot was to be the stuffy twilight of cattle trucks for eternity. My sense of time had become completely confused: I had no notion as to what day of what month it was then. But, as a train crowded with holidaymakers raced past us, it occurred to me that it might perhaps be a Sunday. Bees were hovering about the bushes in front of the station, alighting on the flowers now and again. I plucked a few leaves from one of the bushes – a gesture of freedom associated with the past. It was the first move I had dared to make of my own initiative. A great silence reigned all around, broken only by the buzzing of insects and the soft whispering of the wind. On both sides we were surrounded by bored SS soldiers, awaiting the signal for our departure. I looked around. It must have been a long time since this station was built. Once, I thought, Tröglitz must have been inhabited by ordinary jolly people. On a Sunday like this they would have visited a beer garden, or listened to the music played at an open-air restaurant. Now everything was deserted: there was hardly a soul to be seen in the streets of the village.

Crawling wearily, the line moved on. My neighbor, who knew Germany well, told me that we were not far from the city of Zeitz, in Thuringia, roughly fifty miles from Buchenwald. We had marched for more than half an hour when suddenly a factory emerged before us in the valley. It resembled a huge ship, its chimneys thrust stiffly towards the sky like a ship's masts broken in half. I had seen many factories before, but none as menacing as this one. It sat there in a monstrous solidity, as if awaiting us with a horrible, gaping mouth. The road along which we marched ran past cultivated fields, where grass waved restlessly in the embrace of the wind, and the scent of distant pastures widened our nostrils. How painful was this fugitive fragrance! At last we arrived at a camp – canvas tents surrounded by a fence. A number of savage-looking SS men stood near the gates. As I crossed the threshold, I stumbled. One of them jumped at me and struck me full in the face with his gun, and managed to break my nose.

That was my introduction to the camp of Tröglitz.

At sunset the thousands of prisoners who were already working in the factory returned to the camp. Shuddering, I thought of the time when I, too, would become a similar human wreck.

We stood in *Appel* until late that night. Gradually grey clouds covered the sky, and rain began to drizzle. Our thin prisoners" clothes were soon soaked through; the wind seemed to penetrate our very bones. We just stood there, trembling with cold, feeling that everything had been in vain, that each moment would merely bring death one step nearer.

"Aufsteh'n! Alles aufsteh'n!" (Get up! All get up!)

The night was still dark outside when they woke us in our tent.

"Aufsteh'n, alles auf! (Get up, all up!) Are you waiting for the chambermaid of the Hotel Astoria to come and tap on your door? Get a move on! Are you deaf there?"

We got up slowly from the high three-story wooden bunks on which we had been lying. We were still deathly tired, and it seemed we had hardly put down our heads on the straw-filled sacks before these SS brigands were driving us again. "If ever I get out of here alive, I shall get my own back on these swine!"

"Alles aufsteh'n. You, over there, if you don't get moving you'll get a taste of my rubber truncheon soon, d'you hear? Just because you were a gentleman back home, that doesn't mean you can evade the rules here. You can't play the lord any more: that's all finished...."

The Stubendienst (room orderlies) who had volunteered for this bloodhound's task the night before were fulfilling their duty to perfection, befitting the special occasion of this first morning. The barrack boss was a lawyer from Western Hungary; his assistants were recruited from his personal circle of friends. Truncheon in hand, the former refined advocate was charging up and down the tent, as if he had done this work all his life.

"You bloody bastard ... off! How dare you put your filthy feet on my neck! I'll knock the stuffing out of you, you ...! ... you!" This exhortation was addressed to me. As

I was sliding down from the top bunk I had accidentally touched the neck of my ex-history master with my foot.

"Move on, move on; out you go! *Appel!*" someone was hissing next to me.

"Where's my bread? Someone has stolen my bread ration!" screamed the barber from on top of his bed. His shop used to be on the corner near our house. "I put it right here last night, under my head. Robbers, murderers, you have stolen my bread!"

On the previous night they had handed out a half-pound bread ration to each one of us. With ferocious hunger, I had eaten mine there and then. But the barber had been a methodical person all his life; he had wanted to save some of it for next day.

"Serves him right," said a former hotel commissionaire. "Should have looked after it better. I certainly didn't put mine under my head. And I shan't tell you where I did put it. No, that's the last thing I'd do: or they might steal mine, too."

By now the whole tent was in turmoil. The whistle signal of the SS men rang out shrilly in the courtyard; searchlights were trained on us and the morning line-up began. And each day that we spent in the inferno of Tröglitz started in this way.

The factory in the valley to which we had been drafted was the synthetic petrol factory of the I. G. Farbenindustrie. Some time back in May the factory had been hit by an air attack which had caused extensive damage. But the core of the factory remained alive and continued to produce food for the German tanks and armored cars. Our task was clearing rubble. We had to remove all signs of the devastation, restore the demolished buildings, and bring the whole plant back to working order. It was cruel and grinding work. To force one's body, weakened by starvation, to do fourteen to sixteen hours of relentless physical labor every day, under the constant threat of the SS machine-guns kept trained on us, was certainly no easy task. The truncheons were always busy. We were slaves.

And time, inexorable power, passed with merciless slowness. While we pushed a wagon filled with stones from one end of the rails to the other, our thoughts traveled with the speed of light over thousands of miles to the past, only to leave us even more desperate, more hopeless at the next shift. As we shoveled the sand and watched the heap diminish in front of us, it seemed as though long hours had rolled over our heads. But when we came to check the time, it turned out to have been a matter of mere minutes. No excuse could earn one exemption from labor for even the shortest time.

# CHAPTER VII

In this terrible situation one either worked or perished. Death loomed over us as a permanent threat – and it loosened our tongues, too. People who had guarded secrets for long years, for whole lifetimes, now – in the hours of suffering and mortal peril – confessed to one another.

For some time past an ex-lawyer from Czechoslovakia had been hanging around me during the day. At work, and in the rest-breaks, he always sought out my company. We used to talk about the world we had once known. Already he had related the story of his childhood and the years of his adolescence, until I could almost see before me the small town in which he grew up, the very life on which he had founded his ideas of bourgeois, middle-class security. He also told me of the great conflicts within his soul, of which he had become aware at the time of puberty. It was at that age that Dr. Ekstein had understood something of the reasons that kept his muscles limp and inert; his interests, unlike those of his companions, were not oriented towards women. As time went on he brimmed with ever-growing tension, like a boiler filling up with steam, without the safety valve which would have brought relief. His parents – well-to-do business people – knew nothing of the fierce storm raging in the young man's mind. In the years following his matriculation while he was a student at Prague University, the conflict continued. Sometimes it seemed as if the blood were beginning to throb naturally in his veins at last – but it only happened when he was absolutely alone. Occasionally, as during the solitary hours he roamed about the suburbs, or late at night when in a park he saw the outline of lovers huddled together, he thought that with an understanding woman maybe somehow he could overcome his dreadful inhibitions. But he was afraid; he felt that if he were to be disappointed in a woman of his own, life would lose all meaning and purpose.

Then he met Anna at an afternoon charity dance arranged by the Ladies' Guild. The girl made a deep impression on him as soon as he noticed her. She came from a much more modest family than did Dr. Ekstein; but she disliked superficial dandies, however good the class they came from. Anna was choosy. She was looking for someone in whom the feelings of the human being were not entirely overlaid by the behavior of the animal. Immediately she sensed the boy's unhappiness. Perhaps this was why, in time, she came to love the young lawyer.

At last, after many a sleepless night, Dr. Ekstein made up his mind to marry Anna.

"We spent our honeymoon on the Adriatic coast," the former lawyer continued his story. "We picked a small Italian summer resort called Abbazia, near Fiume. In the evenings we danced together in ecstasy, while down below the sea murmured quietly. But when we returned to our room and to bed, I started to worry again, and I felt as distant from Anna as if the mighty ocean were lying between us. We lay in the dark, hand in hand, without a word. There was, I knew, deep gratitude in Anna's heart. She did not realize that my passivity towards her hid, not consideration for her own wishes, but a sickness that not even our marriage could cure. And so we went on for a whole week. Then, after a sleepless night, I made a momentous decision. I made up my mind that she should be the first person in my life to whom I would tell my secret. It was a Sunday morning, I remember. After breakfast we went for a stroll by the shore. On this particular morning the world seemed exceptionally vivid to my eyes."

Dr. Ekstein turned away from me and stared rigidly before him, as if he was examining the bombed factory and wondering how to start on clearing it up. For a few minutes silence descended between us, broken only by the sound of the wheels of the hand-cart we were hauling at the time, which groaned as if they, too, felt the rigor of slave labor. The contrast between the past of which we had been speaking and the present induced a strange mood of mind and heart.

Dr. Ekstein spoke again. "Then we arrived, Anna and I, at a part of the beach which was completely deserted. We went down on to the warm sand and took off our shoes. Suddenly Anna said she wanted to bathe.

"She threw off her thin summer dress, and there she stood before me, under the blazing sun – naked. Now for the first time I saw how beautiful she really was. As she stood there, at first a little bashfully, half turning away from me, and then ran towards the sea, I felt my eyes filling with tears. Never before had I realized so clearly and mercilessly the extent of my loss. And she was laughing, waving, beckoning towards me from the splashing waves. I sat down in the sand and looked out over the sea, listening to the rhythmic whispering of the waves, a plaintive whispering which echoed infinite sorrow.

"And then I wanted to die. But I lacked the strength and the courage. To die – that demands more courage than it does to live.

"Instead of dying, I found myself neatly folding Anna's dress and putting her stockings into her shoes.

"She emerged from the water and lay down in the sand, resting her head on her arms. She remained there for a long while. Suddenly – without lifting up her head – she said:

"'Alfred, I love you very dearly.'

"And I, trying to stifle my emotion, replied: 'And I love you too, my darling.' Then I added: 'Perhaps you'll never know how much.'

"Anna leaned her head on my lap.

"'I do know how much you love me, you silly thing! Why do you say that perhaps I shall never know how much?'

"'No, not now,' I was saying inwardly to myself. 'I cannot tell her now.' There are some moments which one wants to save for ever. This moment was one like that. Life is so short, and beautiful moments are so rare."

Dr. Ekstein fell silent again. I was beginning to be afraid that I should never hear the end of the story. By then Anna had become a part of myself, too. Her naked body which had been kissed by the sun in Abbazia in 1926 floated like a mirage between the enormous chimneys of the I. G. Farbenindustrie. Amid the whirr of the machines in the factory, above the noise of the trucks knocking one against the other, I could hear her warm, soft voice. Anna was now mine as well as his; Ekstein had no right to shut out this miraculous vision. Tröglitz was unbearable. I, too, needed Anna.

Suddenly the hooters began to wail. Air raid! On such occasions we had to leave the factory in a hurry and return to camp. But still Dr. Ekstein would not speak. When we were back in the camp, we sat down in front of one of the tents. He stretched out flat on his back and covered his eyes; then, as if he had just left off, he went on with his story.

"My hands ran over her wonderfully lovely body. Her breasts stood firm, turning away from one another. A tiny drop of water trembled on her stomach; then, as she drew her breath, it slid down towards the oasis of her thigh. The gentle breeze ruffled the fine down on her legs. It was as though the sun held her in his arms ecstatically – and she opened her body to the sun. When she was dressed, we began to walk towards the rocks. We stopped on top of a hill, and she sealed my mouth with her hot lips. But this was more than I could endure.

"'Anna,' I said, 'I must tell you something.'

"She turned towards me, seeking my eyes.

"'What is it, my darling?'

"'I … I,' I began, but could not go on.

"'What is it, my love?' she asked again and moved close to me.

"'Anna … I want to say that our honeymoon will soon be over, and that the endless, drab everyday will follow.'

"'Of course,' Anna replied. 'Sundays are always followed by working days. But please don't be afraid: I'm not frightened of the working days. As long as you are beside me, nothing can ever scare me.'

"'Anna … I am not a proper man.'

"At first she did not understand what I had said; then, when she did, she tore herself free from my arms.

"'What is wrong with you?' There was fear and deep anxiety in her question. Such solicitude I had never encountered from anybody, not even from my mother. No, even in my mother's eyes I had never seen this expression.

"'O, my God, if you knew, if only you knew what is going on in my mind.'

"Like a small child begging something of a grown-up by tugging at his coat sleeve, she implored:

"'But please tell me, please do: what is the matter?'

"'I am not a proper man.'

"'You are not a proper man? I do not understand.'

"'I do not understand it either, Anna – but I cannot know you as a wife like other husbands. I cannot give you that which other men can. I am not whole.'

"For a few moments she did not utter a word. Then, slowly, something began to dawn in her mind.

"'Is that the reason why you have never made love to me since we arrived here?'

"'Yes.'

"Light and shade played over her face as the clouds alternately veiled and revealed the sun.

"'How long have you been like this?'

"'I don't know. Perhaps I was born that way; maybe I have some organic trouble. God only knows what it is.'

"'Have you seen a doctor?'

"I shook my head in denial. For a few moments she remained deep in thought.

"'Whether you're whole or not, I'm your wife and I love you. If you think that this will make any difference to my feelings, you are mistaken. On the highest summit of love sex is irrelevant.'

"We pressed close to each other. I was in tears as I murmured: 'And I love you, too, my darling. I have never loved anyone as I love you.'

"As we strolled down the hill wrapped in our own thoughts, I was tormented by doubt and fear lest what she had said would become empty words in two, five or ten years' time. What becomes of words when the innocence of youth has vanished?"

Overhead the raiding planes appeared at a great height, bringing us back to the present. Dr. Ekstein and I scanned the blue sky. Those planes above were unattainable links with a world of freedom. In a few hours" time their pilots would be walking on free soil, amused or annoyed as the case might be. Just as we used to do, once upon a time. After the planes had disappeared from sight, the lawyer continued:

"After we returned from Abbazia to Prague, I gradually began to build up a fair practice. We lived without any material worries. In the eyes of the outside world we must have appeared happy – but that outside world rarely perceives the secrets of either body or soul. Although no harsh word ever passed the lips of either of us, the very silence was more eloquent than the most bitter curse. I could not endure Anna's goodness. Behind her words of encouragement I was continually searching for any tone of condescension or self-pity. I was fully aware that I was doing my best to drive away from me this woman who was willing to make the greatest sacrifice possible for my sake, but I could not accept her sacrifice. At times I almost wished that she would take a lover: I thought that might enable us to come nearer to one another. Yet when I reached this point in my thoughts, I realized in a rage of barren desire that I could not endure such a solution, that I would rather kill myself. Secretly I went from doctor to doctor. They examined me from top to toe, and declared that there was no reason why I should not lead a normal sex life. In the end one of them suggested that I consult a psychiatrist. The cause, he said, lay in my mind. But this (God knows why) I could never bring myself to do. So I went on struggling in this horrible, unknown net; there seemed to be no way out for me. On the first anniversary of our wedding day I was so depressed that when we went to have supper at a fashionable restaurant after the theatre, I could not utter a single word.

"At this stage we had already been sleeping in separate rooms for quite a while. But on that night Anna knocked on my door and climbed into bed beside me. For a long time neither of us said a word. I myself found it impossible to speak: she seemed to be considering whether to say what was on her mind or not. At last she spoke.

"'Alfred,' she began, 'it can't go on like this any longer. You are so touchy and you close up like a clam: I just can't bear it. Whatever I say or do seems to displease you. A thousand times I have told you that I can live with you without this matter of sex. But you don't seem able to believe me. You're jealous, and you won't talk. This hellish situation is killing the love between us. It can't go on like this.'

"'What do you want?' I asked bitterly. 'Do you want to go off with somebody else?' I did not mean this seriously. But her reply shook me to my depth.

"'Yes, Alfred. I shall go off with someone else.'

"Before I could fully comprehend the significance of her words, she went on: 'It isn't because I don't love you, or because there's something wrong with you that I'm going away. I'm going away because I want a child. Then at least my life will have a meaning, whether it is with you or without you.'

"She lay there in bed raised on her elbows, her beautiful breasts pressed taut against her nightgown. As if in a trance I stared at her body, which was shaking with emotion.

"'I don't want to become a liar. I don't want to become cheap. I want to go away from you with a pure heart, so that I can come back to you with a pure heart – if you want me to.'

"What I felt then, my young friend, I cannot tell you. I was plunged into the centre of a frenzied whirlpool which dragged me downward and obscured my consciousness. I had never known till then that there was an alternative to destroying oneself: destroying someone else. Madly and impotently I threw myself on her lovely body, my hands tightening round her neck, squeezing out her life, her miraculous, beautiful life. In that moment of wild, ecstatic murder, without any real union of our bodies, a delight which I had never known before surged through my whole being. Then my impotent desire released the floodgates of my tears, and through their veil I saw her lying with her eyes closed, still in the vice of my embrace and strangling fists. Then the radiance of delight poured down upon me again.

"'Anna! Anna!' I yelled, 'Anna!' But she lay on the bed with her eyes closed, her face as pale as the sheet.

"'Almighty God, help me! Anna! Anna!'

"Have you ever had any tragic experience in your life, my young friend? If so, you will perhaps understand what I am going to tell you now. Suddenly the air began to smell. Yes, to smell. This may have been the same smell that assailed the nostrils of the Heidelberg Man when he first crawled out of his cave into the open air – a smell quite unknown to our civilized senses. It can only be sensed by someone who has thrown off the straightjacket of society, and who – in his soul – has regressed through the millennia to an age before history itself. This odor horrified me. Like a madman I crawled to the window to shut out the air. With trembling hands I tore the curtains apart. And then, for an instant, my glance fell into the street. The dim lights of the gas lamps were like a pallid grin. In the middle of the street an old woman was dragging along slowly, pulling a little four-wheeled cart behind her – it creaked rhythmically under its load of old clothes. In the sky the clouds pressed together like demented lovers; the moon surveyed the world in cold indifference. That was a moment of solitude and despair more terrible than any in Auschwitz or Tröglitz.

"I stared at Anna's dead body. Then I covered her up lest she catch a chill, and got dressed and went out into the night.

"I spent twelve years in prison. The judges allowed me to keep my life, but in fact I had already died a long time ago. And now I shall be grateful to the Germans when they kick aside my life like an old rag."

We sat in silence next to one another. The air raid was over, and the whistles that rent the air indicated that we had to return to the factory. I looked into Dr. Ekstein's eyes, and then I could no longer endure his presence. I pitied him. But I also hated him. He had taken my Anna away from me.

# CHAPTER VIII

Until now desire had slumbered within me like life in a cold stone. But Anna's story had stirred me to my profoundest depth. When the all too rare moments of rest arrived, I was quickly sucked down into the whirlpool of sleep, but each time on awakening the knife-edge of desire cut into me. My body cried out for a woman to love. Like an animal shut in a cage, I walked round and round the camp in an attempt to loosen the relentless grip of my desire. Slowly my very soul seemed to split into two; and within it, the longing was divided also. On one side, in hermetic isolation, was the yearning of the spirit, crying for warmth and affection and companionship, of which my mother was a symbol. The other desire was wild and demanding. It howled for naked, writhing women; panted after savage, sweaty embraces. But the two desires were strangers to each other. They came separately, first one, now the other, each in turn making me believe that it alone was sole master. I felt I was going mad.

The menacing, nightmarish factory in the valley; the thud of the SS truncheons; the thousands stumbling towards certain death, acquaintances of yesterday by now almost beyond recognition – all these things added to the mounting compulsion within me to escape.

But how could one escape? Guards were posted at the gate; an enormous barbed-wire fence encircled the whole camp; at each corner a watchtower soared towards the sky, and from it, day and night, soldiers with machine guns watched our every move. And beyond the gate the sons and daughters of an insane nation were ready to victimize any individual who might arouse their suspicions.

But there is one part of the human mind for which the realities of life do not exist. In this dark and wildly spinning abyss escape was possible. First came the dreams. I seemed to be running through endless fields, tired, breathless, perspiring – fields that had no beginning and no end. Sometimes these dreams flooded over into the translucent grayness of the day-time, until it was impossible to tell what was reality and what illusion. I began to view myself as if I weren't myself at all, but someone quite different, as though I were at home, sitting comfortably in an armchair, watching the scenes of some film of which I myself was the hero being projected before my own eyes. "He's getting up. Now he is going towards the latrine. He's watching the guard kick somebody." Yet I was aware of what was happening. I seemed to be attempting to justify this trick of thinking in the third person by the conviction that I was watching scenes from the chapters of a book I would one day write, which made it essential to lower this little curtain between myself and the world. That this book might be written in the first person singular I never dared even to think. This attempt at self-justification showed that somewhere in me there was still a censor powerful enough to keep me afloat on the disturbed surface of normality. But now and again even this censor began to be anxious lest some alien force defy his intervention.

After the dreams came the fears. So far danger had threatened only from without. Now a voice began to whisper in my ears from within. "What if they give you an injection, robbing you of your manhood, making you impotent like Dr. Ekstein?" it said. "What if they render you incapable of uniting your body to those of the women you so much long for? What if you will never be able to father a child? What if … what if …"

One of the obsessive fears of my childhood years had been the image of the robber. The robber, lurking in the dark at night, would wait for Daddy and Mommy to go out of the room … and then he would climb out from underneath the bed … and … and would do something … something dreadful. … Now once again the robber emerged from the distant past. Perhaps this terrifying old acquaintance of mine came in order to lessen, by comparison, my fear of the SS men.

I had never before been superstitious. Now all of a sudden I began to believe in celestial portents which only I could understand, only I could interpret. If on a summer night a shooting star coursed through the sky, it signified the end of the war. If the heavens began to thunder, and lightning clove the body of the night, this meant the savage wrath of God. The crimson disc of the sun at dawn foretold the drowning of our enemies in their own blood. For a while I really believed these to be fortunate signs. Then, when repeatedly nothing happened, I was plunged into an abysmal depression, and felt that life made no sense at all.

How I finally woke up again to the reality of life I do not know. All I remember is that one morning I felt like a color-blind man who all of a sudden beholds the world in its thousand fold real hues. Life regained its meaning anew, and instead of continuing to decipher celestial signs or falling into a deep depression when their deception became manifest, I made up my mind that I was the helmsman of my own fate and that God only helps those who help themselves. It may be that throughout the long weeks when insanity was almost enclosing me, somewhere the decision to escape from the inferno of Tröglitz was forming in my mind. I knew that it would not be easy, and I also realized the risks involved. Yet I knew equally well that there are moments in life when, if one is unwilling to take a risk, death becomes inevitable.

August 16, 1944, started off just like any other day at Tröglitz. The morning *Appel* was a long one, the dawn was cold, and rain began to drizzle. Dr. Ekstein, who in the last few days had again attached himself to me, was discoursing on the purpose of Life and Death. The SS men had been keeping us waiting over an hour already.

Dr. Ekstein turned to me. "Have you ever seen a forest fire?" Without awaiting my reply he went on:

"A forest fire spreads from tree to tree. There's no escape from it: everything is burnt to cinders."

"There is no such fire, in which at least a few trees aren't left whole," I answered.

He stared ahead fixedly.

"Perhaps you're right. Perhaps a few trees will be left over. Perhaps."

We stood next to one another, shivering. By swinging our arms we tried to get our circulation going.

"Have you seen the smoke forming clouds by day, and the flames leaping towards the sky at night?"

"Yes, of course I've seen," I said impatiently. "What are you trying to say?"

"Do you know there are gas chambers next to the crematoria?"

"I do. So what?"

After a few moments' silence he asked, shouting:

"Do you think the Allies know it?"

"And if they do, what does it matter here, to you, to me?"

He shouted back as though he were demented:

"Yes, of course, the Allies know that near Kattowitz people are being exterminated by gas! They have let the whole world know about it. 'How vile! The Nazis are annihilating people by the thousands....' They've enough to spend on propaganda, but not enough for bombs!"

"What bombs is he talking about?" someone asked me, as our neighbors, attracted by the noise Dr. Ekstein was making, began to listen in.

I shrugged.

"The bombs," the former lawyer addressed himself to the questioner, "which they ought to be dropping on these death-camps. I ask you, why don't they bomb the crematoria and the gas chambers? It isn't only I who ask this question. The millions who have become ashes and smoke and flames asked the same thing...." His chest was heaving like a frail boat on a rough sea. "There are enough bombs to go round for every second- and third-rate factory: but not for these slaughter-houses of human beings. Why? Why?"

"Why don't you keep quiet?" someone said.

"Why, of course, they'll have an answer for it. 'We couldn't bomb concentration camps,' they'll say, 'because that would have cost the lives of thousands of people. We stand for democracy. For humanitarian ideals....' But if it is a case of bombing some factory in which deportees are used for slave-labor, then the argument of our renowned humanitarian gentlemen runs thus: 'Why should we desist from hindering the work of the German war machine just because some prisoners are working there?'"

His voice became somewhat lower:

"Had they appeared one night over Auschwitz and laid the gas chambers in ruins, a number of people would certainly have died. But on that same night thousands could have escaped. But they didn't send their bombers; no, they didn't – because they did not want to bomb them." He faced me: "If you ever get back to the world, if you stay alive, ask them why."

The rain had stopped, the SS men came out of their sentry boxes, and the *Appel* was over. Then followed the next item on the daily program: breakfast. For this a few of us dragged the heavy pails filled with some hot liquid from the kitchen to the tents. Then we queued up in a long line and in turn received a helping of this dubious concoction – flatteringly called coffee – in the tin mug we always carried around with us. After "breakfast" we lined up once again. Each person had already been assigned to this or that type of work, so everybody was with his appropriate group. Then there was another lengthy wait for the SS men who escorted us to the factory. This period of waiting was the time when we let our fancy run free. Day after day we would tell one another what we used to have at home for breakfast, lunch and supper. The menus served up in our imagination were a temptation to eye and palate alike. Neither before then, nor ever since, have I "dined" so magnificently as I did during these dawns.

A man called Weiner, a former grocer, was holding forth.

"First of all, about eight o'clock, I got out of a lovely warm bed."

"What did you have as a bed-cover?" enquired Mr. Weiss, a traveler in underwear. The question evoked profound excitement among the members of the group. As if life and death depended on Weiner's reply, every face turned towards him.

"A feather quilt," Weiner answered.

"What did he say?" asked somebody a little farther off who had not caught the reply.

"A feather quilt," his neighbor pronounced the words tenderly. "He used a feather quilt for a cover."

"And then, what happened then?" asked Mr. Weiss.

"I stretched," Weiner continued, "and then I got hold of my wife's lovely warm buttocks."

Not an eyelid fluttered at this breach of good taste. These little details were both important and natural. No one felt that Weiner was committing an indiscretion.

"I loved her buttocks most of all," Weiner stated in a matter-of-fact manner, "because, you see, a woman changes as the years go past. Her breasts don't stand out so firmly as they do in the beginning of married life; her belly gets wrinkled when the children come, but not her buttocks. A woman's buttocks always remain young."

Some were nodding their heads at this world-shaking discovery.

"At eight in the morning Helen was still asleep. Nice and slowly I lifted up her nightgown, and then I grabbed that fleshy arse of hers. During all the twenty years of our married life, every morning she woke up as soon as I grabbed her, saying the same thing each time: 'Leave me alone, you villain. Aren't you ashamed of yourself?' Her buttocks," the grocer went on, "were warm, and her flesh just like velvet."

"And who opened the shop if at eight o'clock you were still playing with your wife's bum?" asked Weiss.

"What's that?" Weiner said sharply. "The assistant, of course. The assistant opened the shop every morning, he did."

"And who dressed the children, and who gave them their breakfast?"

"Look here, I'm talking about these latter years, naturally," said Weiner. "The children were already attending high school; Peter was sixteen and little Susie fourteen. They could look after themselves."

"These were our most intimate moments. When we were younger we made love in the mornings. But, of course, a bit earlier, on account of the children. About half past six. In the winter it was still dark then; we didn't even put on the light. Under the feather quilt it was lovely and warm. In those days Helen's body was like a tiger's..."

Only those who have given up all hope of ever seeing their beloved ones alive again would express in public such details of their private lives, I thought.

"You can say what you like," Mr. Weiss interrupted, "but I say that nothing can give a man such a sense of security, such self-confidence, as a woman's breasts."

"What's that about self-confidence?" asked Biro, the engineer. "Why self-confidence?"

"Please be good enough not to interrupt," retorted Mr. Weiss, angered. "I believe that cosmic energies radiate from a woman's breasts."

"Radiate bloody hell," said the engineer.

"I object to that tone of voice," said the traveler in underwear. "They do most certainly radiate."

"Radiate bloody hell," the engineer repeated.

They had a pretty noisy row over this, and the engineer finally left in a fury, asking what one could expect of an uneducated hawker of underpants.

# CHAPTER IX

It was a beautiful, clear summer day. The sky was blue, but awareness of its infinite depth filled me with a feeling of uneasiness. While I was carrying the cement bags from the trucks to the mixing machine I could not lift up my head towards the heights on account of the burden that weighed me down. But on the way back, walking the machine to the truck, I stared at the sky as though hypnotized. High up there, in that sea of blue, were strange universes, myriads of planets, ever under the eye of a watchful Being. Suddenly the great perennial question of man overwhelmed me: what is the sense of it all? And if I for one cannot comprehend the purpose of everything, is there someone, somewhere, who understands it?

As a child I had been taught by my parents to believe in a God who was encamped somewhere high up in heaven, looking down benevolently upon us all. There used to be a baker's shop in our town renowned for its excellent brioches, on whose walls a host of angels soared above the heaps of rolls, croissants and buns. When on a snowy winter afternoon Mother and I entered the shop, the pleasant warmth and intimate smell of the various kinds of dough gave me the impression that heaven, too, would be full of this lovely, warm odor of bread. In the middle of the ceiling, amid winged, womanish angels, a white-bearded old gentleman of benign appearance spread his hands in blessing over the bakery. This benign old gentleman was for me the personification of God. The existence of God, and the circumstances under which he lived, were in my child's mind connected only with this bakery. That image of God I have carried with me through the years; behind every new impression there lay hidden this early, profound experience.

Later, as I grew a little older, I used to accompany Father to synagogue on Saturdays and on the Jewish holy days. There the grey hair and benign face of Rabbi Mayer Benedict confirmed my belief that God Himself must have been such a benevolent soft-spoken Being. The Rabbi had suffered from some throat disease for many years, and had not preached for a long time. One could only hear his broken, hardly audible voice when he was called for the reading of the Law, or when he spoke to us children as we went up to him to kiss his hand. And seeing that this old rabbi loved children and we loved him, too, somehow I came to feel that God also loved children.

During these whimsical years of childhood, however, God was not exclusively this white-bearded old man. He was also, in some measure, identified with my grandmother. My grandmother was a simple country woman who had brought eight children into the world. Two things earned her a place in my heart. Firstly, her story-telling on Sabbath afternoons; secondly, the fact that she was never angry with anyone. As a small child I used to think Grandmother so good that in her presence I even forgot to be mischievous. There she sat at the head of the table, wrapped in a large red woolen shawl summer and winter alike, describing, in the rich, racy dialect of her part of the country, the world which awaited us on the coming of the Messiah. "When suffering has become like a mighty river," she would say, "and people's tears overflow the whole earth, then, you will see, children, our Savior will come, as it is written in the Book, riding on a fiery chariot from the heights of heaven. And then, as the prophet Ezekiel has foretold it, the dead will arise from their graves and we shall all live for ever and ever."

I was seventeen years old when, after a long illness, my mother died. By that time it was very difficult to envisage God, so I chose her as an intermediary between God and myself. When I prayed, the Hebrew text, most of which I could not understand, meant very little to me. There was nothing in those prayers that could provide an answer to my problems. By merely praising God's greatness I do not know how many thousands of times a year I could receive no reply to the burning questions of my adolescent life. Only once a year did I feel any sense of deep devotion in the synagogue – on the Day of Atonement when, famished and thirsty, and often with tear-stained eyes, people came to implore the Lord of Heaven for forgiveness. But if I was in trouble, all I had to do was to close my eyes, imagine my mother's face hovering before me – and pray to her. Such prayer always gave me comfort and renewed strength.

All affection that I ever received in life confirmed my belief in the existence of God. Love – the love of woman – did so, too. When Eva and I sat on the bank of the Gyongyos River on summer nights, looking at the stars and the moon's crescent reflected in the rippling water, wordlessly holding hands or seeking each other's burning lips, God was there, too. When in the years of my puberty desire leapt up within me, it was He who stood by the furnace, His hands that fed the flames.

Auschwitz had dealt the first great blow to my former belief in God. The thousands of pitiful creatures stumbling towards the crematoria, the hatred and the amorality, the cruelty and death, had unleashed a profound feeling of doubt within me. If all this was possible, if men could be herded like beasts towards annihilation, then all that I had believed in before must have been a lie. There was not, there could not be a God, for He could not tolerate and condone such godlessness. Yet faith, like desire, persists in man.

On the short way between the mixing machine and the truck these thoughts and memories assailed me. And the higher the sun rose towards the zenith of the sky the more restless I became. In the end even my ears were ringing with my uneasiness.

There is an indefinable feeling which throughout my life I have occasionally experienced before events of great importance. Some people call it premonition. I have no name for it. The basic element of this mood is an awareness of sudden occurrence, particularly in the matter of life and death as it relates to myself. How it took root in me, I do not know. Nor do I know to what extent others are aware of the same kind of sensation. But I do know that on that morning, in the midst of my soul-searching after God, I was suddenly shaken by the knowledge that "this was it." All of a sudden I felt that I had to stop in my work. My heart was beating almost suffocatingly fast. Perspiration began to trickle down my forehead, and yet at the same time, in site of the heat of the August sun, I shivered as though an icy current of air had passed by me.

I asked the SS guard for permission to be excused: without a word he nodded. Dizzily I staggered towards a hollow behind the sand heaps and squatted down behind a heap. The sun's rays, reflected upwards by the sand, almost burned my backside. Again I glanced towards heaven. Then I prayed.

"Mother dear, you have always been with me till now; you did not let me perish. I beg you, be with me now also. Something is going to happen, though I don't know what. Help me, Mother."

I calmed down. For a few more moments I watched the sky, and then the silvery grains that glittered in the sand. I drank in the breeze that was caressing me. Tears flooded my eyes. I felt that the die had been cast, that death was crouching somewhere just behind me. But at that moment I drank in life. I felt my mother's presence close to me.

Then the hooters began to wail.

Since May there had been any number of air-raid alarms, but no actual attack from the air. Usually when there was an alarm we were led to a nearby sand quarry or back to the camp. But on this morning the SS decided to keep the group detailed to load cement in one of the shelters in the factory, and while the others were herded out of the camp we lined up in front of the shelter. There a minor quarrel flared up between a Wehrmacht (unified armed forces of Germany from 1935 to 1945) soldier and our own SS guard. The Wehrmacht man, together with a few British POWs, had arrived a few moments before us at the shelter, and claimed priority to it. The SS man was quick to express his opinion about any so-called priority rights of the Wehrmacht in no uncertain terms – to which the Wehrmacht man retaliated by calling the SS man an unprincipled villain. The latter then reminded his fellow-Nazi that the July plot against the Fuehrer's life was made possible by the treason of the Wehrmacht officers, and expressed a hope that the Britons might rot where they were, together with the Wehrmacht. This prompted the latter to exclaim "Let these filthy Jews rot first." Apparently the SS man sympathized with this view, and the way was paved for a compromise, which consisted in both the British and ourselves being given permission to advance into the shelter. First about a dozen of the British were allowed in, then the Wehrmacht sat down between the British and ourselves lest we exchange any words with them, then twelve or thirteen of us moved in, and then the SS man took up his post at the entrance of the shelter.

It was dark inside, the only light coming from the still open entrance. In the background the British sat on the ground, silently drawing on their cigarettes. The Wehrmacht man turned to one of the Britons and, pointing upward, said: "Royal Air Force kaput." "You're kaput," the Englishman said, provoking the laughter of some of his companions.

Such an exchange between guard and prisoner was something new to me. For wretched human pariahs such as ourselves, to answer back was utterly impossible. Had one of us done so, it would have been the end of him, the end of us all. An immeasurable difference yawned between a prisoner of war and a slave.

It was there in Troeglitz that I first saw the British. Occasionally I saw them marching past in a long line between their guards. They walked about the factory as slowly and with as much as dignity as though they had come, not to work, but to a funeral – for whose funeral was apparent from their expressions. In vain did their guards shout at them *"Los, los."* Such yelling left the Englishmen calm and unperturbed. I respected them, and I envied them. My respect was paid to the great nation whose determination it was to bring Nazi Germany to an end, and to the superiority which they preserved even in captivity. My envy was directed at the sons of a land where human freedom was a way of life. Without very much knowledge of England, I could not but sense the assurance of superiority emanating from these soldiers. As they sat there in silence, they demonstrated this to their temporary masters more eloquently than any words could convey.

"I've been in England," said Weiss. "They're an odd people."

"A great people," Weiner murmured.

"They don't like foreigners," Biro said.

"What is there so lovable about foreigners?" asked Weiner, with a gesture of a Talmudist posing the question, "Nu, what is the answer?"

We were sitting in the front part of the shelter, our backs against the wall.

"The English," Weiss continued, "are grey and dull. I spent eight months in London, and all the time I was sleepy. And, believe me, not only because of the climate. Yes, sir, I was there for eight months, and once or twice I was invited to an English home. Well, all the time I felt as though I were sitting on pins and needles. One never knew whether what one did was right or wrong, whether what one said was right or wrong."

Biro, the engineer, looked up suspiciously:

"Do you speak English?"

"Of course I do," said Weiss.

"In eight months one can't learn how to speak English."

"Well, you see, I had already learnt before, at home. Just because I was a traveler, that doesn't mean that I had no education. Many agents have more culture in their little finger than most engineers."

"Well, if you can speak English, translate for me *Lenni vagy nem lenni, ez itt a kerdes.*"

"To be or not to be, that is the question."

"I apologize," said Biro, "you do know how to speak English," and he fell into a mood of bleak depression.

Silence reigned for a few minutes, then Weiner spoke:

"I can't speak English, but I do know that quotation."

Again there was silence. Suddenly Weiner burst out laughing.

"What are you laughing at?" asked Lantos, the jeweler. "What is there to laugh about?"

"A funny story came to my mind," Weiner giggled.

"What sort of story?" Weiss inquired.

"The Professor of English at Budapest University goes on a trip to London, ha, ha, ha ... he gets off at the station and goes over to a policeman. He says 'Pardon me, officer, where is the Hungarian consulate?' The policeman answers: 'I'm sorry, sir, I can't speak German.'"

Weiss showed his appreciation of Weiner's story with a loud guffaw. But Lantos could not see the point.

"Well, and what's the joke in that?" he asked.

"Oh, go away. Once you start explaining a joke, all the flavor goes out of it."

"Don't bother to explain," Biro muttered. "It isn't worth explaining."

This gave them something new to quibble about.

Meanwhile the Wehrmacht soldier got up to stretch his limbs. He strolled over to the SS man and offered him a cigarette as a gesture of conciliation. Then the SS man stood up also. Both of them stepped outside the shelter and scanned the sky.

"You go and ask them," Weiner pointed at the British POWs, "what's the news about the war."

Carefully Weiss looked around. When he was satisfied both guards were outside, he turned to one of the Britons and said something to him. The Englishman politely took the cigarette out of his mouth and indicated that he could not understand Weiss. Biro started to laugh at this. Weiss repeated the question. The British held a brief consultation, at the conclusion of which they threw a cigarette at Weiss, which made Biro laugh even louder. Weiss was enraged and almost shouted at the Englishmen:

"Var, what's the matter with var?"

At last the Englishman understood: "Oh, the war..."

After pondering a while, he said:

"Germany kaput."

"Even I could get that," mocked Biro, who seemed quite ecstatic at the discomfiture of Weiss. "You would certainly have made a fine hawker of underpants in London … ha … ha … ha. …"

By this time we were aware of a steadily increasing humming from above, and within a few moments the distant drone of engines became audible. Shielding their eyes with their hands, the two guards stared into the sky. The Englishmen became listless. So did we. Suddenly there was the sound of an explosion, and the shelter trembled. Weiss, pale as death, shrieked: "They're bombing us; they're bombing us." Then, in his broken English, he screamed the same message to the Britons. It was obvious that our Englishmen were also aware of the grandeur of this moment, but they remained in their places and drew silently on their cigarettes. As Weiss, gesticulating wildly, continued to shout in his own peculiar brand of English, "They're bombing us," one of them quietly said: "They aren't bombing us, but them" – and went on smoking.

What happened then took place in a mere fraction of a second. Something came whistling through the air; a choking silence followed, and then a furious explosion that lifted the roof off the shelter. A sudden, blinding light stabbed into my eyes. I could see the sun above me and the great iron birds flying round and round. What happened to me and to the others during these dramatic moments I do not know. I was only conscious of the fact that wherever I looked I saw fire, and above the fire, jet-black smoke.

When I woke up at dawn and found a snoring woman in the same room as myself, I could not understand it all. The room was already quite light; the clock on the wall was ticking away monotonously. Uncomprehending, I looked at the unfamiliar furniture, straining every nerve to make contact with reality. In the middle of the room, in two armchairs pushed together, an infant was breathing heavily. Immediately over the bed hung a picture of the Virgin Mary and the Child Jesus and just beneath it another of "The Fuehrer." Motionless, my brain awhirl, I lay in the bed and remembered....

When the shelter caved in and I stood among the flames and belching smoke, deafened for some minutes by the concussion, my first thought had been to escape. No one apparently remained in the burning factory. I began to crawl on my stomach along the ground, which was pitted in every direction by craters of ruin and hideous devastation. In one bomb crater which was full of water I washed my face and cooled my aching head. Then, as if mechanically, I tore off my prisoner's clothes and threw them into the flames, and crawled to a wooden shed which had been used by German and other civilian workers as a dressing room. They used to leave their civilian clothes here and change into factory overalls for work. There hung their suits on the hangers, in a neat row. Hastily I put on the nearest suit; then I ran out of the shed. Burning petrol was flowing past near by. I let a piece of wood shaving catch fire, and with it set all the remaining clothes alight. I managed to make my way to the main road unnoticed. No one was about. The raid was still on. By then it was long past noon. Nearby a stone quarry stood deserted, which looked as though it had not been worked for months. There I hid myself until nightfall and as soon as the stars lit up overhead, I set out towards the station. I met many people on the way, but neither my unshaven face nor my crumpled clothes awakened suspicion. The American air raid had swept right through the area, and many people were fleeing in the direction of Jena and Gera. Wherever I looked, there was tumult and confusion. About midnight, the first train rattled in. Because of the air raid an enormous crowd was traveling, so they connected a few cattle trucks to the train. I hauled myself on to one of these trucks. It was dark inside, though while the train was standing in the station, the dim lights from the platform filtered in through the grill of the window. Next to me sat a woman with a small child in her lap. The child was crying. Someone said irritably: "Can't you turn off that alarm clock of yours, comrade?"

"What can I do with him, poor little thing?" She turned to me. And when I took the squealing child on my lap to quieten it while she was arranging her luggage in the dark, she burst into a rapid flow of words.

"You can't imagine how grateful I am to you, I wouldn't know how to get through this dreadful journey alone." Then with a change of voice she continued:

"They cram us into these trucks as if we weren't German citizens of the Reich, but murderers or Jews." Again, she rattled on in a milder tone:

"You know what it is like when someone is left all alone. My husband is serving on the eastern front. Where on earth did I put the satchel with the food? Ah, here it is. He is fighting against the Bolsheviks. He writes to me that soon we are going to win. Oh, I ought to change the baby soon. Do tell me if he wets his nappies. Well, and where did you come from, comrade? Ah, I understand ... from the factory at Tröglitz. Officially, of course ... these days that's the only way to ... of course. The factory has burnt down completely? These murderers, they destroy every factory. Still, there are plenty left.... How long are you staying in Jena? I am going to stay with my sister; she's in a hospital in Gera, as a nurse. Her house is empty. I wired her today to tell her that we were bombed out, so until the authorities make some other arrangements for us I'm moving in there. Please stop pushing, comrade, just sit quiet. There isn't enough room? ... Not my fault. Oh, where was I now?"

Later in the night we arrived. I surrendered myself to my fate, took the baby in my arms, and when I reached the exit, accompanied by the woman, the guard let us pass out unhindered. In the pale light of the station I had a look at her. She may have been about thirty, a little plump, with a pretty face. Her plaited hair crowned her forehead like a wreath.

"And where will you spend the night, comrade, if you haven't made any arrangements? Well ... you can sleep in my sister's house; there's plenty of room. My name," she said, putting all her bits and pieces on the ground, "is Frau Bierbauer – but my friends, and Hans, always call me Hilda. You just say 'Hilda'"; and, laughing, she began to walk ahead of me. At last we arrived. It was a smallish, two-storied house. On the ground floor there was a kitchen and pantry, on the second floor the only large living-room.

"It seems that we haven't got any electricity here either," Hilda said as she turned the switch on and off. "Never mind, we'll light some candles." A match flared in the dark.

Hilda brought some bread, marmalade and margarine, then she went down into the kitchen to prepare the coffee. I fell on the food with savage zest. Somehow or other it reminded me of Cara. She, too, had served me with bread and marmalade and coffee. Outside, the sirens howled again.

A picture of the Virgin Mary and the Child Jesus hung on the wall. Beneath it, Adolf Hitler peered morosely into the darkened room and at the exhausted couple – one of them a Jew.

I awoke at dawn....

Light changes not only the appearance of things but also their significance. In the half-light of dawn, I thought, Hilda would soon notice my close-cropped hair, the hideousness of my scarred body, the ribs sticking out of my sides, my deathly tiredness.

No civilian laborer would ever have fallen into this poor condition, more appropriate to a galley slave. Any attempt at evasion would be a sheer waste of time; I would have to admit my identity. Quietly, lest I woke her, I got up, and a few minutes later I was standing outside the gate, the cold wind of dawn smiting my face. The street was utterly deserted. I began to walk. Every moment I was afraid of someone lifting a weapon against me from behind, as like a thief I scurried from door to door. No matter that I was in the open street, with the infinite firmament over my head, no matter that I could see the smoke rising from the chimneys of the factories, I was still a prisoner. I felt that every step was of no avail, that I was being watched from every window. Everyone was spying on me; everybody a murderer after my life. Round the corner a patrol appeared. I hid myself in a doorway and from there gazed at the steel-helmeted soldiers. They were young, almost children. A few years ago boys of that age were my playmates. The steps grew distant, the deserted street giving back a ghastly echo of their sound.

And now where shall I go? Surely there must be in this great country some decent people who only submit to these evils by the force of circumstances, and who look forward to the end of tyranny? But where shall I seek them? How can I find them in the vast, unknown multitude?

No, it was impossible even to imagine that someone might take me into his house. The Nazi machine worked with the exactitude of a precision instrument. In every house there would be a traitor, in every room someone of whom to be afraid. What I had done was madness. I ought to have rotted away slowly in the Tröglitz factory rather than play this tragic game of hide-and-seek, hungry and desperate, in these dreadful streets. By now I was walking through the suburbs. Here life was somewhat busier. In the factories workers were getting down to their jobs. Perhaps I ought to sneak into one of these factories and start carrying boards or rails. But it would be impossible. "Who are you? How did you get here? When did you start work? How long have you been a member of this group? Who was your father? Your mother? Your grandfather? Your grandmother? Where did your great-grandparents live, and what God did they worship?" Unless I could give the right answers I dared not look for work. How naïve was the notion of the inmates of the camp that anyone who could manage to get out into the streets of the Reich could "become absorbed" into Germany! How hopeless it all was. Perhaps it would be better to go out into the fields and wait for dark there, till work at the factories had ceased. Then I would walk up to the first worker and say to him: "Comrade, you haven't forgotten, have you, the Republic, when there was fighting in the streets against the Nazis? Help me!" But what if he laughed in my face – like the SS man who, during the journey in the truck, laughed at the architect and, smiling, pulled the trigger of his gun?

The open country lay before me, broad fields of green and brown. A little further on, trees were visible. What should my goal be? To reach the trees? And then? To reach into the night? And after that? To reach for life itself?

Once under the trees I sat down on the ground and leaned my back against a tree. The silence was profound, broken only by the twittering of the birds. Up in the sky a fleet of small white clouds was sailing swiftly towards the west, and I wondered whether it would ever reach the free world which existed such an infinite distance away. My solitude was so complete that I felt like shouting out loud in order to hear my own voice. A mild breeze danced playfully amid the foliage of the trees, and through the sudden gaps the sun burst into my eyes with a blinding intensity. I closed my eyelids and in the twilight behind them watched the restless play of light and shade.

When I re-opened my eyes I saw the world reflected in a thousand glimmering hues through the tears which no effort of will could restrain any longer. As though throughout the past months a vast reservoir of water had piled up within me and now the dam had burst, I wept silently there beneath the tall trees.

When, as an adolescent in the course of a fight, someone punched my nose, how ashamed I used to be of the unmanly tears that would well up in my eyes; with what fury I would spring at my attacker, compensating for the weakness of my soul with a show of physical strength. Yet is it always weakness to weep? Now, I felt, somehow this weeping strengthened rather than enfeebled me. It washed away a great deal of bitterness, of suppressed grief; and when at last the tide began to ebb and the waters of my spirit returned to their accustomed channel, I felt young again, a human being once more.

I started to review my situation. Obviously one could not escape the way I had done. Without a map, without documents, without a plan, it was sheer lunacy. If I wished to make for the Swiss frontier, I did not even know in which direction to walk. If I could have counted on a sympathetic population, I might perhaps have taken a risk. But it would be impossible to expect sympathy from such fanatical madmen. I was no prisoner of war protected by international convention. If captured, I might be shot on the spot. And if I ever thought life worth living, I did now. Every hour of life seemed a magnificent gift. I ought to return to Tröglitz. If I could manage to return, perhaps they might spare my life; but how could I risk being caught on the way back? I must give myself up, on the first possible occasion: maybe I could save myself that way. And what if they killed me just the same? Or crippled me for life?

The sun climbed higher in the sky, and obedient shadows moved round with it; I inferred it was afternoon already. There was no time to waste. I had to get back to the camp before nightfall. I made an appointment with the sun. I said to the sun in a low voice, "I'll see you again tomorrow." Like a small child who believes in his own imagination, I awaited the sun's reply. But only the birds were chirping above.

Then I stood up and turned back towards the town.

# CHAPTER X

The police sergeant, when I opened the door of the police station, stared at me as if I had come straight from the moon. He was a big lump of a man aged about fifty, with a fat face. He spoke little, no more than was essential. But God has mercifully given us means other than words for the communication of our thoughts. He has given man the tone of voice behind the words themselves; and the ear which can at times perceive the meaning that a fellow man cannot put into words at all. And he has given us eyes as well, eyes which can see not only the uniform but also the drops of perspiration on the forehead; and the eyes of the other man, too. The eyes of the other man in this case now appeared to be ashamed, and avoided my own. Yes, this fat German, I sensed, was ashamed. Only the two of us were present in his office – or rather, the three of us: Hitler was hanging on the wall. I was thankful that my parents had engaged a German *Fraulein* (governess or nurse) to look after me when I was a child, for I could speak German almost as well as my own mother tongue. I told him the story of my flight. I talked about Auschwitz and about Buchenwald. I told him also the reasons which prompted me to give myself up. When I spoke of the thousands driven to the gas chambers, he interrupted me, saying that this story did not concern him. But at the same time he threw a glance at the Fuehrer, and his eyes said more than he would ever have dared to utter in words. When I had finished, he leaned his large head on his fists and looked out of the window. Then he said:

"I ought to hand you over to the Gestapo...." And again he said nothing for some minutes. I was convinced that although my life, not his, depended on it, he was the more worried of the two of us. He cannot often have been faced with such a problem.

Suddenly he got up.

"Let's go," he said. I asked no questions. I was confident that as long as I was with this big, sweating lump of a man, no harm would come to me.

We walked along the street. I marched a few steps ahead of him, but as we were walking in the road, not on the pavement, even if people looked at us no one spoke to us. At last we reached a biggish building. At first I thought that he had taken me to the Gestapo, but it turned out to be police headquarters. Here he took me to an ill lit room and handed me over to a constable with instructions to keep an eye on me; then he disappeared. The constable now in charge of me puffed away at his cigarette; he did not tell me to sit down, although there was a chair in the corner, so after waiting for about ten minutes I asked if I could sit down. He jumped up as if electrocuted and shouted at me:

*"Schweinejude, Schweinehund,"* (Jew-pig, filthy swine) and swore violently. From this I concluded that apparently I was not meant to sit down – so I sat down.

For a moment he stared at me as if one of us were mad.

*"Bist Du verrückt: Aufsteh'n!"* (Are you mad: Get up!)

I got up again, and, swearing, he returned behind his counter. By sitting down I must have touched the deepest levels of his being, for he proceeded to put his revolver on the table in front of him and shot a meaningful glance at me. Since I myself was not in any position to do the same, I just stood in the corner and awaited developments.

Eventually my sergeant reappeared, together with a higher ranking police officer. Then began one of the most fantastic conversations of my life.

"Ask him," the officer addressed the sergeant, "where he got hold of his civilian clothes?"

This was my cue to turn to the sergeant and tell him that I stole the clothes from a burning dressing room at the factory. Then the sergeant repeated to the officer what I had said as though he were translating it from the Chinese.

"Tell him," the officer declaimed, "that he is lying. Ask him who gave him the clothes."

"The Captain says you're lying," the sergeant repeated, parrot wise. "Who gave you the clothes?"

"I am not lying. I took the suit myself from a burning hut."

Captain: "Where did he spend the night?"

Sergeant: "Where did you spend the night?"

Myself: "In a wood."

Sergeant: "I beg to report he spent the night in a wood."

Captain: "Whereabouts in the wood?"

Myself: "In a wood, I don't know where. I don't know the wood."

Captain: "He is lying."

Sergeant: "You are lying."

Myself: "I am not lying."

And so it went on. The officer asked the questions; the sergeant "interpreted," and each time I waited until the sergeant spoke to me. I felt that this conversation, however painful and in many respects perilous it may have been at the time, would have reaped a terrific success on the stage of a Budapest cabaret after the war.

Captain: "He will be shot dead."

Sergeant: "You will be shot dead."

Myself: "Yes, sir."

Captain: "The SS will tear his dirty bones apart."

Sergeant: "The SS will tear your dirty bones apart."

But as he spoke the words, his eyes sent me quite a different message, as if to say, "Don't be afraid, chum, you'll be all right. The Captain is only having a bit of a lark."

Myself: "Yes, sir."

Then the two of them held a short consultation together. The only word I could discern in their discussion was "Tröglitz." After it, the sergeant came back.

"*Los,* get a move on...."

And I committed blasphemy. I turned to face the captain and threw the challenge between his blue eyes: "Good day. *Auf wiedersehen!* (Good-bye!)"

Whether the gallant captain survived this shock or died of a stroke I never had the fortune to learn. The sergeant pushed me out of the room.

Like a naughty little boy who had run away from home, I was escorted back to Tröglitz by the fat policeman. Neither on the train nor while walking did we exchange a single word. But as we reached the gates of the camp he said, almost casually:

"Good luck!"

"Seventeen," the SS man counted.

The whip slashed down on my bare back. I was tied to a board so that I could not even move; they had stuffed my mouth with rags to drown my shrieks. The SS commander had sentenced me to be whipped for my escape, as an example to others. The punishment was carried out just before the evening *Appel.*

After the first few strokes I thought I could not bear it. I felt blood streaming from my back – as if biting into me, the ferocious lash of the thick whip burned my flesh – like the pressure of iron hands round my throat, something was choking me.

"Eighteen."

Dust ... how the dust glitters in the rays of the setting sun ... surely the earth itself must suffer man's pain? A long time ago ... I am building sandcastles, while Mother sits behind me on a bench. In the park the fountain throws a jet of water high into the air, and on its summit sparkling lights sway hither and thither....

"Nineteen."

Mother, Mother, if you saw me now, your heart would break! So this is what death feels like: such strange tastes gather on the palate; things glow with such odd colors as they glide past, even sounds alter. Oh, I remember feeling this peculiar excitement once before, when I kissed my first girl ... the lamp was burning on the veranda ... and in the garden, the dark night hid the bushes ... why ... why should I did? ... Why? Why must I perish with such horrible pain? Why? Why do all these people in prison uniform just stand there? Why don't they attack these butchers? Why do they stand as if it was no concern of theirs? .... Oh....

"Twenty."

The abyss of darkness draws me down into its yawning depths. Little circles of scarlet dance before me and flash across the firmament. ... Bloody chunks of flesh merge into one another and draw apart, then merge again. Pyramids rise and vanish into nothing. ... I ought to grab hold of something. ... I shouldn't be grasping this man – there's a fire – everything is burning – the fire is burning everything to ashes....

I came to in darkness. It was a strange unreal world to which I awoke. People were talking to one another in every language under the sun. Why was there this noise of Babel in the middle of the night? I was scared of the darkness and tried to sit up, but there was such pain in my body and in my head that after the first movement I fell back helpless. A frenzied thirst tormented me. I thought that my savage screams must rend the night, as I cried to the people around me "Water, water" But no one moved. Then suddenly I had the sensation of being enclosed in a globe of glass from which not even my tormented screaming could release me. This feeling drove me to further panic. Then, after writhing for what seemed like eternity, I suddenly felt a cool liquid trickle down my forehead – "Water" – and one voice rose above the tumult of the rest: "Drink!"

The reviving water caressed my throat and soothed my panic.

"Who are you?" I asked the unknown person in the dark who had given me water and put a wet rag on my brow.

"Dayan Gestettner, my son," I heard the voice from afar, from outside the globe. I stretched out my arm.

"I entreat you to tell me, Rabbi, what are all these voices, why is everybody talking in the middle of the night?"

"I can't understand you, my son. Speak up a little."

"The globe – the globe of glass," I panted.

"He is delirious," I heard the Rabbi's voice. "Poor child, he is delirious."

"Water" – and again he gave me a drink.

"Why is it dark?" I asked after a little while.

"It isn't dark, my son; it is light, it's daytime. We came back from work just a little while ago."

Numb horror arose within me. The globe had broken. I could speak; I could hear, too, quite clearly....

"I cannot see," I shrieked. "I've gone blind."

He did not answer.

"Rabbi," I implored, "they've blinded me."

"He can't see," I heard him say. "He says he's gone blind. Go and find Doctor Danos. Ask him to come here." The man to whom he had spoken said: "I saw him near the kitchen not long ago; I'll go and look for him at once."

"Don't be afraid," the Rabbi said. "Don't be afraid, everything will be all right. You are alive, and that is the main thing." His hand took mine; it was good to feel the slow throbbing of another person's blood.

"They gave you a dreadful beating," he continued, "but God was with you; you have survived it. You will recover. You'll see."

His words eased my mind somewhat. I held his fingers as in a vice.

I was already an adolescent when Dayan Gestettner came to our town to become the assistant of our aged rabbi, Mayer Benedikt. He was a tall, well-built, athletic man, with a black beard. My parents used to speak of the "Dayan" in terms of the most sincere respect, acknowledging the fact that his profound religious convictions did not narrow his mental horizons and that he was equally at home in the Talmud and in the secular, worldly sciences. But, my father was wont to say, what he respected above all in the Dayan was the fact that he was a real human being from head to foot.

The doctor arrived. After examining my eyes he said:

"As far as I can judge under the present circumstances, Rabbi, the eyes are in no way damaged. There is no trace of injury on the face at all. I think that his present blindness must be psychological."

"Thank you," said the Dayan. "Thank you."

He turned to me again:

"You heard what the doctor said. You are not blind; you just don't see. It may be that you don't want to see the world about you, or that you're afraid of seeing your torturers again. But Jancsi, my son, you are not blind."

"I don't understand it," I said, "I don't understand."

"You will understand," said the Dayan. "The time will come when you'll understand it all. But now try to rest. Are you hungry?"

I tried to shake my head, but the movement was too painful. I felt as if my whole body had been torn open by fire.

"On top of the injuries you received yesterday," said the Dayan, "you have a high temperature. That's why you aren't hungry. Go to sleep now. I'll come back to you later, after the *Appel*, and then I'll bring you some water. If possible, I shall sleep here next to you tonight."

"Thank you, Dayan."

Then I was left alone. Open-eyed I lay on my bunk, staring blindly into the private night of my own. Terror lashed at me, rising and falling, and each time it did so I could feel the mad racing of my heart, and my whole body became drenched in perspiration. All I wanted was to drink incessantly – but there was no one to give me a drink. Outside, the *Appel* had begun. Only an infant alone in a dark room, thirsting for his mother's warm milk, could feel so utterly lost.

Then the snowball of memory started to roll downhill, gathering in its passage long forgotten images so clear and lifelike that each one made me feel as though the past had really come to life again. As a rule, our memories come to us in the form of pictures, and we are fully aware of the gulf between the present and the past. Sometimes, when the memories are exceptionally vivid, tastes and smells also are carried over into the now from the then to add flavor to the images. But it only happens rarely that one becomes completely part of the past again, with a veil drawn over the present, and sees with the actual eyes of childhood. What I felt during these feverish moments I had never experienced before; never had I lived the past as intensely as I did then.

Somebody is putting me down on a table. Above me hangs a large chandelier: a torrent of light from it is pouring down on to me. Moths are fluttering around the lamp. Everything is moving – the chandelier sways, the whole room quakes, shadows and patches of light tremble on the walls. Suddenly from my lungs comes a savage yell of fear – and then, with a firm hold, someone lifts me to herself. Her nearness calms my frightened trembling: after the unwelcome cold, warmth flows through me. There is nothing to be afraid of now, I am not lost – I am alive....

A new image appears.

"Good night, Mari. Don't forget to put the child to bed in good time."

"Good night, Madam, Good night, sir."

"Where are you going, Mommy?"

"I'm going with Daddy to the café. Mari is going to look after you."

"Don't go, Mommy; stay with Jancsi."

"We'll be back before you have time to turn round, my little boy."

"But I don't want to stay with Mari."

"Good night, Mari."

"Good night, Madam."

Her elbows on the table, Mari is reading the newspaper. I am lying on the sofa, feeling very depressed. It is evening; a summer evening. The windows of the veranda are open; the fading glow of the sun just set provides a gloomy backdrop.

Mari is reading the paper aloud: "Afterwards the murderer hid the corpse in one of the store rooms at the theater. It was only discovered some days later...."

"What does it mean, 'Murderer' Mari?"

"Shut up."

"What is a murderer, Mari?"

"A man who kills people, that's what it is. Now keep quiet."

"Does a murderer kill children, too? Mari, does a murderer kill children too?"

"Of course he does. Now shut up!"

"Why does the murderer kill children?"

"Cos they ask too many questions. That's why...."

Silence. Mari has finished reading the newspaper. She looks at me.

"Yes, that's it. It's printed in the paper. The fellow killed his lover and then hid the dead body...."

"What's lover, Mari?"

All of a sudden Mari is in a good mood. She sits down beside me on the sofa and giggles:

"You'll be a lover too one day, young man."

"What is a lover, Mari?"

"You'll know when you grow up, don't you worry."

Mari has thrown herself back and is now lying across the sofa.

"Women are very fond of lovers, Jancsi – very fond. Mari likes lovers too. And how!"

Her skirt has slipped up to her thigh.

"Pity you aren't a bit bigger, young man. A great pity. I just happen to feel like a lover right now."

"I'll grow up, Mari, won't I?"

"That you will. You'll grow up, but by the time you'd be any use to me, I shall be a dried-up old woman ... ha ... ha ... ha ..."

She begins to rock herself on the sofa, from side to side, backwards and forwards – then suddenly she picks me up and draws me to her.

"You little man, you...."

She is hugging me so tight that I can hardly breathe.

"Come ... show Mari you love her ... stroke Mari...."

A little later Mari says:

"If you dare tell a word about this to Madam, I shall kill you. With this knife. Promise you won't tell.... Promise, you shitty thing."

"I promise."

"If you talk, the doctor will come and kill both of us. Do you understand?"

"I understand."

"Swear on it. Swear on your eyes. Say "I swear"

"I swear."

"I swear on my eyes."

"I swear on my eyes."

"You know what will happen if you break this oath? You'll go blind. You won't be able to see."

"Yes."

"There now – off you go to sleep."

Now it is a Sunday afternoon. In the park with Mari, walking towards the woods. "We are going to meet Laci. Laci is as strong as a bull. Don't jabber too much, or Laci will kick you so high that you'll never come down."

Laci: "What the bloody hell did you bring the brat along for?"

Mari: "I couldn't have got away otherwise. But don't worry. We'll send him off to play."

Laci: "Perhaps he'll see something and start talking at home."

Mari: "Well, let him talk...."

Mari and Laci are walking away towards the trees, leaving me by myself. "Don't you dare move from here! You know what will happen if you go away?"

"I know."

"Well, what will happen?"

"I shall die."

I can hear the voices of Laci and Mari. They are struggling behind the bushes. Laci is killing Mari and after that he is going to kill me as well. Yet I dare not run away. I am afraid that I shall go blind.

It is months later.

Mother: "That girl is worse than the lowest whore."

Father: "And her eyes looked as innocent as a lamb's! But she was a toothsome little morsel, one must admit!"

Mother: "Ernest!"

"I hope she did no harm to the child." Then, turning to me:

"Did Mari ever do anything to you?"

"No, Mommy, she didn't."

"She never hit you?"

"No, Mommy, she never hit me."

"Mari was a very, very bad girl."

"She was, Mommy."

At this point the images faded and the past returned to the past. Once again I became aware of the reality of Tröglitz. I sank into a deep sleep.

True to his promise, Dayan Gestettner came back later on. He had brought me some water, too. Then he lay down beside me, and from memory murmured some Hebrew texts under his breath. This Talmudic chanting brought me back to my senses, back into this world. It was evening. Outside, the light of the setting sun fell scarlet on the tents. Minutes had passed before I noticed that I could see once again. And then I remembered how, in Jena, I had arranged an appointment with the sun. Now I had turned up at the rendezvous.

"Dayan...." I turned towards him, "I can see you again."

"I prayed for you, my son. God did not forsake you."

And then I wished I could tell the Dayan about my experience with Mari, and all the horror of the past that had been awakened within me. I wanted to tell him how my fear of becoming blind had lain dormant within me ever since that episode, and how all through my life so far I had been expecting the punishment for what I had done to Mari when I caressed her body on the sofa. With their savage beating, the Germans had shocked into consciousness this fear within me, and this had caused my temporary blindness. But I could not bring myself to tell all this to such a clean-living, saintly man. I was afraid lest, outraged, he would turn away and leave me by myself.

All through that evening Dayan Gestettner spoke to me of the greatness of God. I listened to him without a word. But I felt that God was far, far away from me.... Mari was much nearer.

# CHAPTER XI

I made a slow recovery. My persecutors allowed me to lie on my bunk, and my fellow prisoners brought me soup and bread and water. Some of them stole my food, others did not. Those who cared for me remained human beings in spite of the prevailing barbarity.

Apart from Dayan Gestettner, Dr. Ekstein was closest to me during these critical days. Late into the night he would sit there on the bed next to mine, imparting strength and solace by his every word and gesture.

"Somehow I believe," he said, "that one day you will return into the world of free men. Will you be able to forget everything you've experienced? Are you going to be embittered, broken and disillusioned – or will you have enough strength to find a purpose and meaning in life again?"

I could not answer him.

"Those who live through these concentration camps," he continued, as though to himself, "will become one of two types. One type will turn against society, with a completely selfish disregard for everyone except themselves. They will say: "I have suffered; now let others pay for my sufferings." These will become oppressors of the future, unhappy tyrants, whether as heads of families or as employers or as lovers, or in any other of life's myriad roles. The other type of man surviving all this will be more humane than ever before. He will have learnt here something that no other form of education could have taught him. He will have learnt the value of life, his own and that of others, and the worth of freedom, too. These, who will throw in their last atom of strength on the side of justice and truth, will become the martyrs of tomorrow and possibly also its saints."

He stopped for a while, then continued:

"Jancsi, lad, what do you think determines the destiny of a person? What does it depend on, whether one is dragged down by suffering, or raised to a higher level by it? What decides our fundamental sensitivity or insensibility? Biochemists attribute it all to the hormones; psychologists to early and unresolved conflicts; sociologists put everything down to poverty and unsatisfactory working conditions. Have a look round. How many of these people did you know back home? Quite a number. Of the good ones, how many have remained good? And how many of them who used to be bad have become human beings here? The concentration camps have created a civilization within a civilization. And in this new civilization the truths and laws whose validity we believed in for centuries have been turned upside down. I ask you, Jancsi: if you compare these two 'civilizations,' don't you find yourself compelled to conclude that the people who under these abnormal circumstances manage to prove themselves human are not necessarily those who can do so outside the prison bars? And if you can see an answer to this problem, tell me: on what does it depend whether a man remains a man?"

After a few moments of silence he went on:

"As I was saying, many of the good have become bad, and many of the bad have become good. But it is the personalities that have changed, not the values. The Good remains good even here; and Evil, evil. Out there I once killed a woman, but here I could not raise my hand against anybody. I could not steal even if I had to perish of starvation. I committed murder, I sinned – but I am not an absolute murderer. The crime which I committed did

125

not make me a criminal for my whole life, even though I realize that I had to be punished for it.

I was born a Jew, and nothing could have forced me to forsake the faith of my forefathers, even though religion meant little to me. Yet during the past few weeks the feeling has been ripening within me increasingly, that behind these never-changing, eternal values there hovers the inscrutable spirit of an Everlasting Being. And here, in the wake of all this suffering, both within and without, I begin to understand the true meaning of Christianity also. Fettered by my impotence, I did not realize that my whole being was not impotent. As if hypnotized, I could see only one thing: my own sexual problem. My whole life revolved around this – and an innocent woman had to die because I could not tell the wood from the trees. But now I feel that I know the truth. The impotent man is not the one who is incapable of having a sex life, but he who cannot receive God into his soul." He turned towards me and smiled. It was the first time that I had seen Dr. Ekstein smile.

I was taken aback by this complete and sudden change in one who had so recently said: "I shall be grateful to the Germans when they kick aside my life like an old rag."

"What has happened to you all of a sudden?" I asked, almost stammering.

"All of a sudden?" Again he smiled. "There was nothing sudden about it, my young friend. But the realization comes suddenly. Throughout our years of despair, these aspirations lie dormant within us, unrecognized."

He quoted the New Testament:

*And seeing the multitudes, he went up into the mountain; and when he was set, his disciples came unto him;*

*And he opened his mouth, and taught them saying,*

*Blessed are the poor in spirit: for theirs is the kingdom of heaven.*

*Blessed are they that mourn: for they shall be comforted.*

Tears had gathered in his eyes.

"I am no longer young; I have little hope of ever getting out of here alive. I no longer want to die, but my strength is ebbing away; before long I shall be gone. But I am not afraid of life any more, and so I am not afraid of death either."

Suddenly he grasped my hand.

"Thank you for having listened to me at the time when I needed to speak. My confession helped me to achieve this 'sudden' recognition, as you put it. I believe that we human beings live not only next to one another, but in some way also within one another. When I am dead, I shall be merely a memory for you. Yet, after a fashion, I shall be living on in you."

From this time I began to stand on my feet again, though dizzily and feebly at first. But as time went on my strength returned, and with strength, my will to live as well; until one day, early in September, I went back to work. At first I felt so exhausted and giddy that I did not think I would last out the day. But at last the day came to an end.

When we had finished our work for the day, we had to wait in groups before the large gate of the factory for the SS guards to escort us back to the camp. Not far from the entrance to the factory, in a smaller building, worked the typists and secretaries. It must have been some perverse impulse which drove these German girls to the doors of their offices to stare and giggle at our misery. Years ago they used to show madmen on Sunday afternoons, serving them up as circus exhibits to a public hungry for amusement. We, too, were now a circus exhibit: starved to the bone, bald, filthy, denuded of even the appearance of humanity. And there stood these young girls and women, pointing at us, laughing at our exhausted despair; laughing when someone fell down; laughing when the SS kicked the fallen man; and laughing when, weeping, he rose only to stumble again. The SS men appreciated to the full the beauty of the situation, and beat us with added zest for the entertainment of the ladies. Some of these pretty young women made gestures towards us of vulgar significance; others lifted their skirts above their knees, swaying their legs and hips in the hope of arousing our unappeasable desire. But by then, towards the evening, we were too tired to feel anything.

"If ever I get out of here," one of my younger companions said, "I shall crawl over all these bloody whores – and then I'll throttle the lot."

"I shall take an SS whip and beat their bodies to a pulp – their naked, rotten bodies."

"I'll kill them, and let them rot away where they are."

At this point Dr. Ekstein interposed:

"Blessed are they which are persecuted for righteousness' sake: for theirs is the kingdom of heaven."

"Bloody nonsense," said the young man, "Absolute, bloody rot. They ought to string up every single Christian bastard. The Christians are responsible for all this wickedness."

A few nodded their approval.

"Christ died on the Cross," the young man went on, "and what have they been doing in his name? Inquisitions; murders by the thousands. The Church is the greatest enemy of mankind. They ought to exterminate the lot of them after the war."

"Exterminate, exterminate..." said Dayan Gestettner, "Why keep on exterminating all the time? Hasn't the time come to start building something at last?"

"Rabbi," he sneered, "you are lying. In your heart, you're lying. Don't tell me that you could forgive these harlots. This murderous, bloodthirsty mob. This rotten, buggering German people. Your sort have lied from the pulpit, lied in your private lives. Now your sun has set. A new world is being born, without priests and murderers."

"You've just said that these thugs should be murdered," I interrupted. "So how can you talk of a world without murder?"

"To kill Germans is not murder, it is delousing."

"That is exactly what the Germans say about the Jews," said Ekstein.

"You'd better shut up – you're talking nonsense. Spineless, collaborating swine, that's what you are...."

The lines of waiting men jerked on. We marched back to camp. I was so tired that I could not even queue up for my supper.

Summer that year was a short one. Autumn came early, and with it the rain poured down incessantly. The damp penetrated us to the bone; in our thin wet clothes we were shivering all the time. Death waved his scythe, too, as one after another people fell ill and died.

One of the tents, known as "Revier," was crammed with dying people at that time, among them Dr. Ekstein. According to Dr. Danos he had caught pneumonia, and for three days he struggled, half-conscious, against death. At the end of the third day, at the start of the Jewish New Year, he took his leave of us. There were no dramatic farewells; no moving words were spoken. This would have been impossible in any case, since he did not regain consciousness during the last twenty-four hours. I stood there beside him while they undressed him. "A dead man doesn't need clothes," they said as they carried them off. Someone had already stolen his shoes. As he lay there naked he seemed so small, so insignificant. But later, in my memories, he was full of significance.

# CHAPTER XII

At the end of September they made a list of the sick, the SS men telling us that whoever was prevented by illness from working would be taken back to Buchenwald for hospital treatment. In vain did the Polish prisoners (who in the course of several years had had ample opportunity to learn the tactics of the Nazis) utter their warning that in Germany slaves are taken, not to hospital, but "into the smoke," and that the sick convoy would be taken back to Auschwitz and not one would survive. Some of the Polish prisoners were even prompted by their awakened human conscience to use physical force in order to stop the younger ones from volunteering. But the majority of the newer arrivals would not believe them, and there were many who asked to have their names put down.

In spite of this, I put my name forward. I felt there was no choice. I knew that I could not stand another winter in Tröglitz and that I would die if I had to stay there. On the other hand I felt somehow that once I was in Buchenwald I might be able to survive.

Rain was falling, and we stood in long lines before the Tiger (that was the nickname we had given the camp commandant). We offered the most serious diseases we could think of: cancer, tuberculosis, anemia and so on – for the Tiger was only interested in the dying. There was no medical checkup of any kind. The Tiger accepted our words at their face value.

If they had had any hair to tear, the Poles would have been tearing it now.

"You bloody sheep, you fools, do you imagine for one moment the Tiger believes you? He is only willing to accept a Jew's word when he is pronouncing his own death sentence."

But their words were of no use now, and at the end of September we were ready for the journey.

We spent that last night in a tent specially reserved for this purpose, which no one was allowed to leave. In fact, the SS men threatened to shoot dead anyone who either entered or left the tent. But since there was no guard outside, I sneaked out late at night and looked for the few who had been my friends to say farewell. Dayan Gestettner again warned me against the possible consequences of my hasty step. But when I remained intransigent, he gave me his blessing, murmuring the ancient formula of our faith with his hands resting on my head:

"The Lord bless thee and keep thee; the Lord make his face to shine upon thee, and be gracious unto thee; the Lord turn his face unto thee, and give thee peace."

When, in the morning, the gate of the camp closed behind us and I cast a last glance at my comrades awaiting the *Appel*, I was thinking: Shall I ever in my life see them again?

It was several years before I received the final sad reply to my question.

In Buchenwald our quarters were in the Zelt Lager, the tent camp, where we had also stayed on our arrival from Auschwitz. Apart from the morning and evening *Appel*s we had nothing at all to do. We lay about on our bunks, or roamed idly around in the area surrounded by the barbed-wire fence. We were forbidden to leave the Zelt Lager, but the prisoners of the Upper Camp could occasionally pay us a visit. Although we still wore our striped prisoners' garb, the inmates of the Upper Camp were going about in civilian clothes, and were generally better clad and looked after than we were. The camp police, recruited from among the prisoners, tried to maintain order in a uniform which might have come straight out of an operetta. Under the circumstances they behaved quite humanely. It was also a unit chosen from this camp police that stood guard over us by the gates of the tent camp.

Within a few days of our arrival in Buchenwald new transports arrived, and among them were many former citizens of my own home town. Meeting again gave us a great deal of joy. These new arrivals gave us an account of our acquaintances, both the living and the dead. Sadly we worked out how many had perished in so short a time.

It was in the Zelt Lager (tent camp) that I met Sandor Sauer, father of my childhood friend Tibi. He was in very poor health. Yet this man, whom we used to nickname Sour Joe at home on account of his embittered, tight-lipped manner, became a perpetual optimist in the concentration camp, assuring everybody that "whatever anyone may say, we're going to live to see the end of the war in good health and strength."

The news broadcast on the BBC reached us before every *Appel*. How it reached us I do not know, but it was a fact that we were always well-informed about everything. It was whispered that there was a secret radio set inside the camp, and that some of our comrades spent day and night listening to it. (At a later stage this rumor was confirmed.) After a fortnight of doing nothing, there came the news that a medical examination was about to take place in the camp cinema, and that the sick would then be sent to hospital. Once again the whispered propaganda spread a different version: the sick and those unable to work would be taken to the gas chambers. But after the two weeks of rest in Buchenwald, during which our provisions had been both ampler and better than during the time of our most severe labor in Tröglitz, no one would listen to these rumors.

By then I had completely recovered from my injuries and my exhaustion. Food and sufficient rest had restored my nerves, and I felt much better than at any other period during my time in concentration camp. Once or twice they even took us to have a hot bath. We were given soap, too. Some people hinted that the Germans manufactured the soap from the fat of murdered Jews, but to me this notion appeared too fantastic even to consider.

Thus strengthened, both physically and mentally, I awaited the medical examination. I had decided to put on a great act of feigned sickness. Tuberculosis, I thought, would be my best line: the doctor could not detect it by a purely external check-up, and in any case I had been told this medical examination, too, would be very superficial.

We assembled in the Buchenwald cinema in which occasionally in the evening they would put on some ancient German films for the benefit of the prisoners. Of course this cinema was a cinema only in a secondary capacity. Its primary function was as a sorting house on a large scale, where the groups of prisoners were parceled out to different slave labor camps. It was from this cinema that we had been dispatched to Troeglitz at an earlier stage.

At the time of our first stay in Buchenwald every prisoner had been given a prison number which he had to sew on to his prisoner's uniform. My own number was 64725. Now, in the cinema, the members of the camp police copied each number on to a slip of paper. When each man came to be examined, he was to hand over the slip to the SS physician.

We made ourselves comfortable on the cinema seats and waited for our turn to come. The seat next to mine was occupied by a young fellow who spent the time of waiting quoting poems by the major Hungarian poets. He expounded his theory that some of our poets could hold their own by international standards, and that "the great Hungarian tragedy" consisted in the fact that, because we were a small nation, the outside world did not know our poets.

"Take Mihaly Babits, for instance," said the boy, whose name was Bandi. "Well, I'd like to bet that Babits's translation of Dante is better than the *Divina Commedia* in the original.

"How can you judge?" I asked. "Have you read the Italian original?"

"Of course I've read it," said Bandi, a little hurt. "I have been learning Italian for six years. I read the Italian papers as easily as the Hungarian ones."

He swallowed hard.

"And don't you see, the same thing is true not only of Babits but of the work of other Hungarian authors, too. Among the more recent one, the Villon poems of Gyorgy Faludy are infinitely better than the original."

"Faludy," I said, "did not translate Villon but re-wrote him. In his Villon poems only the root idea belongs to Villon, the actual poem is Faludy's."

"But these poems, old chap, are better than the original."

"Can you speak French, too?"

"Of course I can. I used to have a French governess as a child. French is a second mother-tongue to me."

Our neighbor, whose leg was swollen to elephantine dimensions, interrupted us.

"What's wrong with Hungarian literature is what's wrong with the Hungarian people, I should imagine. It hasn't got a voice or a flavor of its own. Whatever is good in it is borrowed from the West. It's a matter of imitation, sometimes skillful, other times clumsy. Ady, our greatest poet of the twentieth century, is no more than a rehash of Baudelaire or Verlaine."

"I beg your pardon, but you take that back," said Bandi. "How can one even say such a thing? That is why there is anti-Semitism – because Jews can be so blind. Of course there is a considerable, genuine national literature." He proceeded to quote a dozen Hungarian authors and poets, until our lame neighbor beat a diplomatic retreat.

"All right," he said, "there is a national literature. Have it your way. But let us forget about literature for a moment and talk about architecture. Budapest, my friend, has not a trace of any national characteristics. The whole town was designed and built after the pattern of Paris. Just have a look at the Parliament building." With his raised arm he pointed in the direction of the crematorium. "It is neither chalk nor cheese. I would call it a crossbreed, a bastard architecture. A mixture of Gothic and Baroque. Whatever you say, my friend, Budapest isn't a Hungarian city, but a bit of Paris and a bit of Sofia." Bandi and the man with the swollen foot would no doubt have come to blows over this had not the queue advanced and we moved up a row; and since our lame friend could not keep up with us, we lost sight of him. Our new neighbors were not interested in either Hungarian culture or architecture. They were discussing whether the Germans ought not to have allowed at least the able-bodied members of a family to stay together. Even ignoring all humanitarian considerations, from a purely practical point of view that would have been the right course of action to follow. A man who has his wife with him works more efficiently than one separated from her.

"Now if I were Himmler," said a man called Blau, his breast swelling for a moment, "I would have set about solving this problem in the following manner. Number

One: Husbands and wives who are both able to work should be kept together."

Another man: "But my dear Mr. Blau, what if they did not want to be kept together?"

Blau: "How do you mean, not want to?"

The other: "Just not want to. Period. I myself, for instance, am thankful that I don't have to see that old witch of mine with her endless nagging. If this whole business weren't quite so uncomfortably hard" (then he corrected himself) "so -----ing hard, I should even be grateful to the Germans that at least I am free."

Blau: "You're an idiot. What d'you mean by saying you're free?"

The other: "I'm rid of the old witch, so I am free."

Blau: "You are a fool. Couldn't you have got rid of her without the Germans?"

The other: "No."

Blau: "Why not?"

The other: "Because I couldn't."

There was silence for a moment.

Blau: "Well, as I was saying. If I were Himmler, I would have kept together those husbands and wives who wished to say together. Secondly ..."

The other: "And where would they have lived? Where would you, my dear Mr. Blau, have lived with your wife? In the crematoria?"

Blau: "How do you mean, where would I have lived?"

The other: "I mean just that, where? Where would you have stayed? Would you have allowed your wife to sleep in the company of a thousand other men?"

Blau: "I said you were an idiot. What d'you mean by a thousand other men? My wife wouldn't even have looked at one other man apart from me."

The other: "And the thousand other men would have obligingly shut their eyes ... eh, ... when you and your wife went to bed, or into your little nest, right here in the Zelt Lager?"

Blau: "God have mercy on you. You haven't an ounce of imagination. Of course, the other thousand men would also have their wives in their little nests, as you put it."

The other (after a lengthy pause): "And how would a thousand men see to it that no accidents happened?"

Blau: "What sort of accidents, you fool?"

The other: "Well, I suppose these thousand men would occasionally sleep with their thousand wives. And what would have happened if some of these thousand women, let's say a hundred, found themselves in the family way, eh? What then? Off they go at once to the gas chambers. Didn't you think of that, you half-wit?"

Blau: "I hadn't thought of that."

The other (softening): "Do you see...."

Blau (slapping his forehead): "I've got it. Contraceptives."

The other: "Contraceptives?"

Blau: "If I were Himmler, it would be worth my while to provide the family with French letters."

The other: "Really you are a blockhead – and you are not Himmler."

By now I was sitting in the front row and thus had an orchestra-stall view of what was taking place on the platform. The SS doctor asked each man what was wrong with him, then folded up the slip of paper with his prison number on it, and placed this on one of three heaps. I noticed that two of these heaps of paper slips had increased to a substantial size, while the third contained hardly any.

So far the SS doctor had been sitting with his back towards me, and I had not been able to see his face. But when my turn came and I stepped in front of him and looked into his face, a cold shiver ran through me. It was an infinitely inhuman face, narrow, with a tall forehead, thick brown hair parted on the side, tight lips and a thin nose. But it was the eyes which scared me most.

"The eye is the mirror of the soul." These eyes did not mirror any trace of a soul. The brown color merged into the unusually large black pupils which, when they were looking at you, seemed to be seeing not you but something else. There was something in them that recalled the eyes of a wax figure, as if their every blink were produced by some mechanical process. When I say that these eyes were inhuman, I do not mean it in the usually accepted sense of the word: they were simply non-human. Had I been introduced to this doctor as a newcomer from Mars or Venus, as a typical Martian or Venusian, I could well have believed it.

During the fraction of a second that my eyes met his, only my unconscious mind was working. My conscious self wished to tell him that I had tuberculosis, but in fact I answered his question by saying I had an inflamed bladder.

Mechanically he repeated:

*"Blasenentzündung."* (inflamed bladder)

*"Jawohl, Herr Doktor."* (Yes, Mister Doctor)

His hands reached out for my slip of paper and without taking his eyes off me he dropped it on to the small heap.

*"Abtreten!"* (Withdraw!])

I was convinced then that my faltering tongue had cost me my life, for I was certain that the small heap signified death. For two nights I did not sleep, asking myself why I had not said tuberculosis. I thought that the doctor must have seen through my malingering, and that my fate would not be the hospital but the gas chamber. On the morning of the third day my answer came.

All inmates of the tent camp were lined up for *Appel*. Then we were surrounded by a cordon of the camp police and one of them read out a list of numbers. Each man whose number was mentioned fell out of the line and was given a large chunk of bread and a whole tin of meat, happy to have been chosen. Here and there I could recognize an acquaintance. Sandor Sauer, Bandi, Blau and many others. These lucky ones would be going to hospital. They would be looked after; they would be well off. Fewer and fewer of us were left in the group still standing in *Appel*. In the end only six of us stood there idly.

Six of us were left alone in the large area of the Zelt Lager. The rest had been taken to hospital – to a chance of life. We would soon be going to our death. The gate of the camp had been shut, and the minutes dragged by. All of a sudden a man came stumbling from the latrines, holding his stomach and moaning. He was moaning both because he felt sick, with blood in his diarrhea and convulsions of cramp, and because the transport had gone and left him behind although he was really ill and in need of treatment. He wept and beat his head with his fist, then he dropped on the ground, writhing with pain.

The hours passed slowly as seven of us waited for our end. At last it was time for the evening *Appel*. Seven of us stood there for *Appel*. The man with the cramp in his stomach implored the SS man to let him join the others.

The SS soldier grinned. Then he said:

"The others aren't alive by now; or if they are, it won't be for long."

Next morning we learnt from the inmates of the Upper Camp what had happened to our comrades. They had been put on a train in the forest of Buchenwald. Eighty to a hundred men, the really ill and malingerers alike had been packed into each truck. Then the trucks had been sealed. For a whole day the sealed trucks stood there in the forest, then they rolled off towards Auschwitz.

My "inflamed bladder" had saved my life.

The remaining seven of us were taken over to the Upper Camp. First of all we had a bath, then we were disinfected, and then they took away our striped prisoners' clothes and gave us instead much warmer, quite decent garments. After that we were marched to Barrack No. 23, known as the Jew-Barrack.

This barrack, like the others in the Upper Camp, was divided into two parts: a living-room with tables and chairs; and the dormitory, with double bunks and sufficient blankets for every man. Next to the entrance were the wash basins and the lavatories. We ate our food off plates, with spoons and forks. We could even shave. So, compared to Auschwitz and Tröglitz, the Upper Camp at Buchenwald was a veritable paradise.

Solidarity and equality were the watchwords at the Upper Camp. Certainly there was less thieving than in Auschwitz where, by the time the food reached us, it could hardly be called food at all, to such minute proportions had it dwindled. Here food was shared out in a relatively honest fashion, on a basis of equality. Everybody was equal and a comrade, even if some were slightly more equal.

It was the Communists who were in charge of the offices, kitchens and barracks; here, as elsewhere, these jobs involved certain advantages. These comrades constituted the elite of society at Buchenwald, with their secret cells and secret meetings – which were known to everybody. When they spoke to you, you could not help being aware of the honor which they seemed to be conferring on you. You had to watch every word you uttered. Although you were theoretically free to say what you liked, you could not avoid a certain feeling of uneasiness. After the elite came the middle class. This consisted of other, non-communist, political prisoners who were under suspicion by the Communists, who regarded them as "unreliable". The Social Democrats had betrayed the working class, therefore they were untrustworthy. The other bourgeois elements had been the lackeys of capitalism as long as they could, and were now only reaping their well-deserved harvest. The political prisoners who came from the Church were not merely untrustworthy, but downright dangerous. The ranks of the lower middle class of Buchenwald society were filled by prisoners transferred from German gaols – homosexuals (although those who became homosexuals in the camp could and often did belong to the aristocracy), jailbirds, thieves, murderers, as well as members of the sect of Jehovah's Witnesses. Then came the proletariat, those prisoners who were brought here purely because of their Jewish racial origin. Members of the upper class and the middle class wore a red triangle beneath their prison numbers; the lower middle class were resplendent in black, green and mauve; a yellow triangle adorned the proletarian bosoms. The POWs of various nationalities belonged to different categories; the respect accorded to each was determined by their nationality.

The Germans had set up the concentration camp of Buchenwald in July 1937, on top of the Ettersberg, near Weimar. From the summit of this mountain one could look down into the fertile valley where life, once upon a time, had run in normal channels. Here, on the peak of the Ettersberg, in a profound silence broken only by the twittering of birds, a large oak had once stood in splendid solitude. The great German poet Goethe used to come here; and it was not very far from here that he composed his immortal poem:

*Wanderer's Nachtlied*

*Über allen Gipfeln*
*Ist Ruh,,*
*In allen Wipfeln*
*Spürest du*
*Kaum einen Hauch;*
*Die Vögelein schweigen im Walde.*
*Warte nur, balde*
*Ruhest du auch.*

**The Wanderer's Night-Song**

*O'er all the hill-tops*
*Is quiet now,*
*In all the tree-tops*
*Hearest thou*
*Hardly a breath;*
*The birds are asleep in the trees:*
*Wait; soon like these*
*Thou too shalt rest.*

Even during the building of the camp – done mostly by prisoners – death had taken a heavy toll. In the early years the corpses were taken to be incinerated at the Weimar crematorium, but when the number of the dead continued to rise, Himmler decided that Buchenwald should have its own crematorium, and before long one was erected. Incineration took place in two big ovens, with a capacity of ten to eighteen corpses at a time.

The first political prisoners who had shown opposition to the German National Socialist Party were brought over from the camps of Sachsenburg and Lichtenburg. Later, their number was inflated by hundreds of German Jewry. Insufficiently fed and clad, these prisoners had to rise early in the morning and work at a stone quarry outside the camp until late at night. Certain other groups were put to building roads. The rate of mortality was colossal, and people died one after the other, not only on account of physical weakness, but also as a consequence of the brutal cruelty of the SS men. One of the amusements of the SS consisted in forcing the exhausted prisoners to haul enormous, heavy lumps of rock from the quarry to the camp, many miles away, only to fetch these loads back to the quarry next morning. Many, unable to bear this life any longer, brought it to an end by feigning escape in order to be shot dead by the SS. During those days the total number of deaths per month exceeded two hundred – including, of course, those who were beaten to death or shot dead.

According to my fellow prisoners who had been in Buchenwald from the very beginning, the SS did not only commit these brutalities themselves, but also compelled those prisoners who were in a supervisory capacity to do the same.

After the assassination of Von Rath, advisor to the Paris Embassy of the German Reich, 12,500 German Jews were dragged to Buchenwald. Within a short time the majority of these were murdered with almost incredible cruelty. A hundred of them became insane the first night, when the SS indulged in an orgy of brutality. Some of them were set alight, alive, by a flame-thrower, to run up and down like living torches within the cordon of the laughing SS men.

After the German occupation of Austria in March 1938, the deportation of political prisoners and Jews from Austria to Buchenwald began. It was here that they killed, among others, Winterstein, a former Austrian Minister of Justice; Trummer, the directing superintendent of Austrian prisons; Heilmann, the Social Democratic Member of Parliament, and many other eminent writers and politicians.

On November 9, 1939, in the *Burgenbraukeller* in Munich, an attempt was made on Hitler's life. That same night the SS picked out twenty-one Jews at Buchenwald and killed them on the spot. Another twenty-one Jews – who, of course, knew nothing about the matter – were told to volunteer for what was described as "interesting work." They were taken to the quarry and made to carry huge stones backwards and forwards until at last they collapsed. Then they were shot dead.

From those beginnings, as the Germans invaded country after country, the population of the camp increased, and the mass murders, committed with diabolical refinement that defies imagination, assumed astronomical proportions.

In the course of time I came to know some other details as well. During the war many SS soldiers had to be transferred elsewhere to exercise their butcher's skill, and so gradually the running of the camp slipped into the hands of prisoners. The Reds managed to take over more and more of the key positions, and eventually succeeded in creating a comparatively orderly life within the camp. At last the SS came into the camp only for the *Appel*, in order to count the prisoners, but otherwise they were not often to be seen within the electrified fence.

I soon learned that I was being observed. As we chatted informally, my Communist fellow-prisoners seemed to be trying to find out all there was to know about me – my past, my present, my lovers, everything. When they found out that my father had once been a Social Democrat, they gave me up in despair.

Nevertheless, I felt that I was a human being once more. Best of all, I had the opportunity of making other friends who had no ulterior motive beyond that of friendship.

# CHAPTER XIII

The leaping flames had shrunk into glowing embers in the large iron stove as darkness settled upon the sick-room of *"Buchenwald's Revier."* I had been laid up there with dysentery for the past week. In the first few days a high temperature had robbed me of both the strength and the inclination to move; but now, in spite of my fever, I was feeling better. In this relatively small room, on double bunks, about fifty sick men lay, suffering from dysentery, typhoid fever and pneumonia. Death was a daily item on the agenda. The dead were left to lie on their bunks until nightfall; when it was dark, they were carried to the crematorium. It would have been ludicrous even to think of methods of hygiene. They did not change the sheets on the bed where a man had died: there were no sheets to change. A patient suffering from tuberculosis would be shoved into the bed of a comrade who had died of typhoid fever, on to the filthy straw which reeked of vomit and bloody excrement. We hardly ever saw a doctor. Treatment, in all cases, consisted of being made to swallow, morning and evening, some white stuff that made most of us vomit. Those very seriously ill could not, of course, eat anything: they just took a taste of the porridge-like pulp we were given for meals and left the rest. The convalescents, on the other hand, were always hungry, and finished up anything the others had left. Occasionally these convalescents managed to collect rations for those who had just died, pretending that they were only "asleep." A prisoner, a German homosexual, was in charge of our ward. He soon became accustomed to the groans of the dying and the screams of those in pain, and in his dirty "white" coat would sit reading quietly by the fire-side. If the noise of suffering became too loud, he would bawl out, "Shut up you..."

Once in a while an SS doctor would pass through the Revier. On these occasions the old inmates, however badly they were suffering, tried to sit up in bed and give the impression of men well on the way to recovery. They told us that it would be from here that the SS doctors would pick out the guinea pigs for their various experiments. The chosen ones would be transferred to another barrack, Block 46, where they would be injected with typhoid bacteria so that the "doctors" might study the effects upon them. It was rumored that completely healthy people, too, were killed in Block 46 in the course of such experiments – a rumor that was later proved to have been true.

Slowly the fire went out altogether in the large iron stove, and black silence descended upon the ward. Most people, exhausted by fever, were sleeping. But sleep seemed to avoid my own brain. Despite my temperature I was experiencing a peculiar sense of well-being that had no justification in reality. Then, slowly, in wave after wave, sexual desire began to course through me. Restlessly I started to toss about on my bed. I tried to think of something else, of my dying fellows, of my own hopeless misery, of the crematoria of Auschwitz belching their smoke by day and fire by night towards the heavens. But my thoughts were drawn back each time to the desire that was raging in my body. The smoke of the crematoria became a symbol of my own torment; the fire by night represented the fire of my own lust. So greatly was my desire stimulated that I began to imagine I heard the laughter of women panting with ecstasy in the dark. I tried to stop the sound by covering my ears with my palms. Then I realized that when I did so the women's laughter had ceased. I took away my hands and again I heard their disturbing laughter, and now and again the sound of raucous male voices also. No. This was no more imagination. These sounds could only have come from the camp brothel. There were no other women in the area of the camp.

"D'you hear them?" my neighbor asked. "Our comrades, and the SS men, the bastards, enjoying themselves. Do you hear it?"

I did hear it. And I saw it, too. I saw those women in the arms of men savage with lust; I saw their enticing, writhing bodies.

"I can't stand it any longer."

Louis turned round in his bed. "One can stand a great deal, my friend; a very great deal."

My voice came with difficulty: "I don't know what's happening to me. I feel as if I had taken some drug. I'm completely confused."

"It's the drug of life that's working in you, my friend, the opiate of life. One week in bed, and life must out."

"Louis..."

"What is it?"

"You are a writer, Louis, aren't you?"

"Hmmm."

"Tell me, Louis, which is the more fantastic: reality or fantasy?"

He was thinking aloud:

"Both. Both of them are fantastic. For a writer, both are important. Only madmen live in absolute fantasy – and they cannot create. And only those who are spiritually barren can live in absolute reality: they cannot create, either." He sat up in his bed. "I believe that anything that is imaginary can, given the right circumstances of space and time, become reality. Jules Verne's *Journey to the Moon* was a fantasy then, in his time. For the age following our own it may well be reality. Reality is founded upon fantasy."

"Louis, may I tell you one of the most beautiful, sad, and fantastic events of my whole life? What I am going to tell you is absolutely true."

And I told him of my marriage in the asylum, and of all that had happened up to Eva's death.

For a long while Louis was silent. Then he said:

"Don't think only of what you've lost. Consider what you've gained. There are few people in the world who really love and are really loved. Even for a few hours."

"Yes, Louis," I said, "I know." I buried my face in the putrid straw and wept bitterly.

For a long time we lay listening to the silence and the groans of our companions, and to the sounds coming from the brothel. But I was no longer tortured by desire. The memories and the tears had washed it out of me.

"How would you feel," Louis said suddenly, "if you knew that the woman you loved was being embraced by ten or twenty men every night? Not because she was a nymphomaniac, but because she was being raped. And you couldn't do a thing about it."

"A dreadful thought," I said. "Dreadful."

"The reality is more dreadful."

"For God's sake, Louis, what are you talking about?"

"A little while ago you said that you couldn't stand the sounds coming from the brothel. What would you feel if your own woman was laying there, at the mercy of those men?"

A cold shiver ran through me. I thought Louis had lost his reason. He must have sensed what I was thinking, for he said:

"You must think I am mad; but, alas, I am not. The woman I love is at this very moment lying there, with her body open to those brutes."

"In the brothel?"

"Yes. There."

He propped himself up on his elbows in his bed. In one corner one of our comrades was murmuring the Lord's Prayer in Polish. Somebody cried out for water, then silence reigned again.

"You've honored me by telling me the tragic story of your marriage. Now let me tell you about my love affair with Claire.

"I am a writer. And when I say I am a writer I am not only speaking of my profession. I am a writer in the way I live. I must express what I feel, I cannot do otherwise. If I ceased to be a writer, I would go mad, or die. I am also a husband, and the father of a little girl of six. I love my wife and I adore my daughter. But Claire I do not merely love; I simply cannot live without her.

"When a *maquisard* shot and killed a German soldier in the rue de Clery, the Germans threw a cordon round the whole area and deported most of the people in the neighborhood. That is how I got here.

"So, when I walked in through the gate of this camp, I said to myself, 'All right. Here I am. I shall have a look at the life here. And one day I shall tell the world what I have seen.' As I said, I am a writer.

"And I did have a look at everything; and what is more, I saw it all, too. I saw the transports arriving; I saw the ovens of the crematoria, and the gallows in the courtyard. I saw what I could, and I penetrated to the core of people's lives. It was all very exciting – up to the time when I went along to the brothel.

"I must be frank with you. I missed making love very badly. But I did not go to the brothel in order to make love. I could not make love to a prostitute. I went simply because the brothel was part of the life of Buchenwald.

"You know that only with the consent of the hospital and on payment of two marks can one get a ticket to the brothel. Well, I got the ticket. I told the doctor the reason why I wanted to go there. He understood.

"Claire was lying on the bed, her eyes closed. She was wearing a transparent slip, and nothing else. I told her to put on some clothes because I wanted to talk to her.

"'Talk?' asked Claire, without moving. 'I don't want to talk to you. Do what you came to do, and get out.'

"She pulled up her slip and her body stared at me in utter nakedness.

"As she lay there with her eyes closed and her body offered for my embrace, the blood surged to my head.

"'Put on your dress. I don't want to lie with you. I am a writer and I want to talk to you.'

"She went on laying there, her eyes closed.

"'Don't talk so much, you writer, you. This is a hell of a time to talk. Why do you make the thing more difficult than it is already? Come on and get it over.'

"Claire was young; her skin was white as snow. Her long black hair fell untidily over her breasts.

"By this time my muscles were tense to the point of snapping, and my brain was in ferment. I threw myself upon her white body. I was utterly mad at that moment. And Claire lay cold and motionless as a statue.

"When I recovered my senses I began to implore her to believe that that was not what I had come for. But she just lay there on the bed. She did not even look to see who it was that had embraced her.

"'Look at me,' I entreated, 'look at me.'

"'Why should I look at you? What difference does it make?'

"'Look at me, I beg you, we are fellow-countrymen. I can't leave here until you have at least looked at me.'

"Then she opened her eyes and looked at me coldly!

"'I've had a look at you,' she said, and turned away from me.

"An immense despair overwhelmed me," Louis continued.

"I had never before experienced such despair. I would have given my life to get Claire to believe me or to indicate, even by the merest glance, that I was not just one of many hundreds of men to her. But she just lay there on the bed, turning away from me.

"Then my madness reached its peak. I reached into my pockets where, in a matchbox, I kept a few razor blades. As if she had sensed even through closed eyes the act of madness I had committed, Claire suddenly turned round in the bed and looked at the blood trickling down on to the floor. Then she looked into my face and said with profound contempt:

"'Must you mess up my room as well?'

"That is how I got here, into the Revier. I almost died after my attempted suicide. Why this blind love for Claire ever arose in me I don't know, nor the reason why I wished to die. What I do know is this: until the day Claire becomes mine of her own free will because she loves me, life has no meaning."

In silence we lay next to one another. I could say nothing. I did not understand this kind of desire which aimed at self-annihilation. Is a man incapable of bearing the cross of self-deception? Could Louis not face up to the fact that all he desired was merely an embrace? And when he caught himself red-handed in wanting that, why should he want to die? Was it because it is easier to accept death than the truth? What motivates our will? What forces use us as pawns in their savage, senseless game? What is the answer?

Louis whispered to me:

"Speak to me. For God's sake say something, or I shall go mad."

# CHAPTER XIV

I came out of hospital restored to health. I am convinced that I was cured of my illness not by any white stuff (which in any case I only took occasionally), but by my immense yearning to live. I was taken back to Barrack Number 23, where I managed to get myself work in the inner area of the camp, in the so-called Bau III. My work consisted in carting bricks on a wheelbarrow from one place to another, without any rhyme or reason. The work was light and supervision was negligible. Not far away there stood a small hut in which our foreman spent the whole day brewing ersatz coffee for himself, whiling his time away by reading. His green badge indicated that he was a criminal. He was known as "Gustav the Gangster."

Gustav the Gangster was a bald, round-faced man of about fifty who refused to say what had brought him to Buchenwald. According to some he had once robbed a bank and had been transferred here from a German prison years ago. Others suggested that Gustav used to work for the British Secret Service and had stolen some important papers from the German Foreign Ministry. Whatever he may have been, one thing was certain: He had no love for Jews or Communists.

He would describe at length the manner in which Jewry had brought this war about, saying that the only grounds on which the Germans could be forgiven were the extermination of this Judeo-Communistic menace. Personally, he said, he had never had any grudge against any individual Jew; and from a humanitarian point of view he deplored all that they had to suffer. Yet what was happening was, in the ultimate reckoning, right and proper; and the world would be a better place without them.

As he elaborated his plans for the de-Judaizing the world, Gustav offered me some of his coffee. According to Gustav, the invisible threads that tied me to World Jewry still made me a contemptible rascal.

"What sort of invisible threads, Gustav?"

"Invisible threads. That's all."

He took a big gulp of the bitter ersatz coffee.

"That secret society, the worldwide secret society of the Jews, of which you're also a member. Don't tell me it isn't true; I know for a fact that at the age of thirteen every Jew is initiated as a member of this secret society. From that time onwards he starts working to destroy Christendom – just like the Freemasons or the Klu Klux Klan."

At first I attempted to argue with him and explain to him that at the age of thirteen years a young Jew is recognized as an adult person, and not admitted into a secret society; that the overwhelming majority of Jews have become assimilated into the country in which they dwell; and that although I belonged to Jewry in a religious sense, my forebears had lived in Hungary for generations and I was primarily a Hungarian. But no argument was of any avail. While I talked his eyes narrowed as he searched for hidden meanings behind my words, and then he smiled quietly to show that he knew full well that whatever I said was in any case untrue, one of my "secret oaths" having been the obligation to deny the truth unto death.

So I gave up arguing with him, realizing that in his case the Jewish problem was a pathological symptom which did not stand or fall by rational considerations. Otherwise he behaved decently enough towards me, and he allowed me to come into his hut as often as I wanted to warm up. It was bitterly cold at that time, snowing incessantly by day and night.

One day the whole Danish police force of Copenhagen arrived by coach, having refused to co-operate with the Germans. They were housed in the barracks near the Zelt Lager, and the discipline and good conduct of these new comrades of ours quickly earned the admiration of us all.

I made a new friend among them by the name of Niels Ahlmark. He managed to survive, and later returned to Copenhagen.

Niels and I walked a great deal together along the uneven, potholed streets of the camp, telling one another about the past and present, discussing the future. From his Red Cross parcels – which I, being a mere pariah of a Jew, was not entitled to receive – he gave me nourishing food, butter, jam, chocolate. And what was more important still, he literally clothed me from head to foot, underwear included. Without these warm garments it would have been very difficult to get through the icy winter at Buchenwald. When I thanked him for his gifts, he merely replied: "It is not necessary to thank me, but if you wish to repay, give in your turn to others." I owe to him the restoration of my tottering faith in human beings, and even in humanity itself. I should like him to know how much I cherished and valued his friendship and his true Christian humanity, and how often I thought of him during the hours of my subsequent vicissitudes, and at the times when in my own humble way I "repaid" what I had received from him. Of my comrades then only a few are alive as I write these words, but through the mercy of God Niels Ahlmark is alive and works again in the police force of Copenhagen. I am sending you now, Niels, the benediction of our ancient faith, which expresses what I felt towards you in Buchenwald, just as I do today:

The Lord bless thee and keep thee; the Lord make his face to shine upon thee, and be gracious unto thee; the Lord turn his face unto thee, and give thee peace."

The longer I stayed in Buchenwald the more acutely conscious I became of the growing restlessness among my comrades. Once in the course of conversation Niels said: "We are sitting here on top of a volcano about to erupt." How right he was!

Everybody was well aware that as the front-line drew nearer and nearer, the SS, cornered, might resort to a desperate last expedient and slaughter us to a man. We citizens of Buchenwald all realized how unstable the equilibrium was on the summit of the Ettersberg as we saw, day after day, the condition of the prisoners who streamed in, already tortured nearly to death by the Germans. We knew that Zero Hour would come and were prepared for anything.

Perhaps it was this anticipation of Zero Hour which compelled the Communists to suggest a compromise with the non-Communist political prisoners. Accordingly, after the evening *Appel*, shadows could be observed scurrying from barrack to barrack, as preparations were begun for the payoff. According to a whispered rumor, a considerable amount of arms had been gathered and was at the prisoners" disposal, but would only be used as a last resort. Groups were formed to patrol the camp at night and to give warning of any SS men who might be in the area of the camp and about to swoop down on us suddenly. In one of these night vigils I, too, participated, without knowing at all clearly what it was all about. But everything was quiet in Buchenwald.

It was rumored that a "Comrades' Court" was also operating in the area of the camp, accusing, and passing sentence on Kapos who had returned from Auschwitz and other camps, as well as other prisoners holding office in camp, on the count of crimes against humanity. It was also whispered that some of these murderous Kapos had already been executed by our comrades.

The loudspeakers installed in the barracks, which during the day played military music and relayed the news from the Fuehrer's General Headquarters, spoke of "hedgehog positions" and "tactical withdrawals." But through the BBC, we were well informed of the truth behind such German Nazi catchphrases. Yes, the front lines were slowly crumbling. The Nazi war machinery was in general retreat. In the East and in the West, the German losses were gigantic. The end of the war was no longer a dream, as it had appeared in Tröglitz.

If someone were asked: "Tell me, when exactly did you grow into a man?" he might answer with natural surprise: "How can I answer such a question? Growing up is a slow process. It doesn't happen suddenly, say, on the third of December, at half-past twelve – it takes place during one's whole life." Maturing is a gradual thing, yet within its slow process one can pinpoint certain hours or days or weeks, of which a man may rightly say that this or that event contributed to his maturing.

My own adolescence came to an end in Buchenwald, in a dramatic and very definite way.

As long as I can remember I have never been anything but a second-class citizen of the land where I was born. Despite the fact that according to documents my ancestors were Hungarian Jews as far back as the seventeenth century, and many of them engaged in agriculture – an occupation supposed to be untypical of the Jews – I myself was always discriminated against on account of my origin, and often by people whose own descent as Hungarian was questionable. In the course of time this feeling became manifest in the form of an inferiority complex; and this sense of inferiority was apparent in a desire to excel over others, to "show 'em," out of sheer spite, that I could rise above the ordinary level. I had never considered the motives behind the urge for self-expression, or the problem of creativity. If there is a talent lurking inside one, does it materialize from the depth of the soul under certain circumstances only, or is it inherited from ancestors and does it find a channel for its expression under any circumstances whatsoever? The question is prompted by the fact that during my adolescence I wrote poems, the majority of which appeared in print. In fact, in the part of Western Hungary where we were living I used to be known as "Heimler, the poet." My first volume of poetry was published when I was seventeen, on the very day the war broke out; the second appeared in 1943.

I always felt that I had to be better than others; that I had to "show the world" that I was not merely not second-rate but even better than first-rate. I was convinced that I had to answer to the world: it was only in Buchenwald that I learnt that I had to answer, ultimately, to no one but myself.

It was in Buchenwald that I learned, from Jews, Christians, Moslems and pagans, from Englishmen, Serbs, Rumanians, Czechs, Frenchmen, Belgians, Dutch, Russians, Greeks, Albanians, Poles and Italians that I was only one more suffering insignificant man; that the tongue my mother taught me, and my Hungarian memories, and the traditions of my nation, were nothing but artificial barriers between myself and others. For essentially, as Mankind, we are one. A slap in the face hurts an Englishman as much as it does a German, a Hungarian or an African. The pain is the same; only our attitude to the pain differs, according to the culture pattern of the country and the individual. Our dreams, each dreamt in a different language, spell out the same dream in the language of Mankind: all of us want peace, security, a life free from fear. And, each in our own way, irrespective of differences of nationality or race, seek for the meaning – or meaninglessness – of life and death, believe in God or deny Him, cry for a woman on whose bosom we may rest our tormented head. I also learned that it is a fallacy that there are great nations and little nations: there are merely nations which occupy a large territory and others which have less land. Greatness and smallness can exist side by side in any nation, just as they do in the case of individuals. This in its turn taught me to understand the pointlessness of ambition for the sake of fame or success, because as I was I was neither worse nor better than others. During the long walks in Buchenwald with Niels or Louis, I learned to understand that it is only through the grace of God that I am not a murderer like Dr. Ekstein, only through His grace that I am not impotent, or in love with a prostitute, like Louis. I learned that within me, as in others, the murderer and the humanitarian exist side by side; the weak child with the voracious male. That I am not in any way superior, that I am not different from others, that I am but a link in the great chain, was among the greatest discoveries of my life. From then on I resolved to support those who fell, even as I had been supported. When someone was despicable, greedy and selfish, I remembered all the occasions when I, too, had been despicable, greedy and selfish. Buchenwald taught me to be tolerant of myself, and by that means tolerant of others.

It may be that I would have learned this without the lesson of Buchenwald. But I would have learned it much later – perhaps too late.

"What will be the first thing you'll do when you're free?"

"I shall go to the biggest restaurant I can find and eat right through the menu – everything on it."

"I'll pick up a little floozie and spend three days in bed with her."

"I shall go to church and kneel down before the altar."

"I shall look for my wife."

"They killed my child. I want a child."

"I shall sit down in a big library, the kind that has a glass roof, and read a book."

"I'll go to a night club with a bit of skirt, and get tipsy."

"I'll get married."

"I'll find the man that reported me to the Gestapo and beat the life out of him."

"I shall rape every German bitch I can find in front of her husband."

"I shall have a memorial stone set up for my parents who were killed."

"I shall move in with my sister. Mother always used say 'Don't leave one another.'"

"I'll have a hot bath."

"I'll eat a bucket full of ice cream."

"I shall have treatment for my TB."

"I don't know what I shall do."

# CHAPTER XV

On the December 13, 1944, I was drafted into a transport known as "Transport Schwalbe" heading for Berga-Elster. I said good-bye to Louis, wishing him good luck for his future, to Niels (who gave me his entire Red Cross rations as provision for my journey), to Gustav the Gangster, and to all my other acquaintances. Everybody commiserated with me as though I were going to my death, for outside transports were considered even more dangerous than Buchenwald. I felt certain that I was going towards life. And when in the morning the large gate of the camp closed behind me and, with a parting glance, I read the inscription "JEDEM DAS SEINE" – To Each His Own – I smiled. My lot would be life. It must be so.

At one time there used to be a factory at Berga-Elster. But the machines had been dismantled and the enormous shed fitted with wooden bunks to accommodate the two-thousand strong contingent of prisoners which had recently arrived at the new camp.

It was a cold winter sunset as, standing in *Appel*, we waited to march into the former factory. Outside the iron gate the dimmed lights of the little town were twinkling. All around gigantic, snow-covered mountains stood in frozen grandeur.

"Still, one day spring will come," I thought as I looked at them, "but will I still be alive when the mountains of Berga-Elster don their green cloaks?"

Through the gateway I scanned the street. On the station building opposite a large electric clock showed the time: half past twelve.

The inaccuracy of the clock made me nervous. If a man can watch the passing of the minutes he can endure his fate more easily. But this clock did not stir. It was as if the paralyzed hands were telling me:

"This is the end of you. Time died at half past twelve."

"If ever I get out of here, I shall submit a resolution to the Hague, demanding that all clocks in prison camps shall henceforth be kept in working order. It is inhuman to display a clock that has stopped in front of prisoners. The station master ought to be tried by a People's Court."

At last we entered the factory area which, from then on, was to be our home.

Maxim Gorky would probably have been abashed to know that in comparison with this place his own "Night Shelter" was a luxury hotel. The cold misery, the starkness of the wooden bunks and the vast emptiness of space between roof and bunks brought tears to my eyes.

As I stood there, looking at the turbulent confusion created by my two thousand fellows as they rushed towards the bunks, the steamy exhalation of their breath swimming like a mist before my eyes, I noticed something that jolted me out of my own misery. In the corner next to the big door three frightened-looking children were standing, hand in hand. They were probably about ten or twelve years old, but from the appearance of their thin, shivering bodies they might have been no more than six or eight. They stood at the edge of the seething crowd; huge tears streamed down the face of one of them. I went up to them.

"Who are you?" asked the weeping boy. There was a tense silence. Fear had stopped even the tears.

"Don't be afraid of me," I said in German. "I want to help you."

Silence. Then, hesitating, one of them asked:

"Why do you want to help us?"

My voice choked in my throat. "Why should I want to help you? Because," I wanted to answer, "because you are even more helpless than I am. Because you are alone, because you are children. Because, by the grace of God, I am still a human being."

"Why do you want to help?" asked the child a second time, searching my eyes suspiciously, aggressively. "Leave us alone. Go away!"

An image rose suddenly before my mind's eye. A winter evening. I am perched on my father's knee; he is "giving me a ride." Rhythmically he jogs his knees up and down, then – hopp-la – he lets me drop between them, holding me with his strong arms to make sure I don't really fall. The ride is repeated, to uproarious laughter. Then father lifts me up high in the air and hugs me to himself. I can feel his stubbly chin, smell the bitterish odor of cigarettes, and I am aware of the wonderful feeling of security that radiates from this big man, the feeling of love directed to me, his son. I know that he would never allow me to fall. Never...

The image faded. The three children stood before me, their teeth chattering.

I took the weeping boy, who was called David, by the hand. "Come along." At first he resisted. But I was stronger than he was. "Come along." He came with me, and the two other children followed.

We had not moved more than a few steps when I saw that there were no longer four of us, but seven. The new additions were adolescent lads of about fourteen or sixteen. But they, too, looked frightened. By the time we had reached the middle of the shed, fifteen children surrounded me. They just stared at me, speechless.

Then, suddenly, a sixteenth one – a Russian boy called Ivan – came up to me. In halting German he asked whether I was responsible for the children.

I answered "Yes," without knowing why I did so. But in that moment all feelings seemed to affirm that I was indeed responsible.

It was only some hours later that I began to understand why these prematurely aged children had clung to me. They had been misled by the Danish military uniform which Niels had given me. They thought I was someone of importance in the camp, specially entrusted with the care of children. For in Buchenwald there had been a definite policy regarding children, inaugurated by the Communists. It was not for humanitarian reasons alone that the Communists had concentrated their efforts on these children, but also for purposes of indoctrination. They had stored their minds with Marxist-Leninist ideas, because they were to be the Communist youth of the Spartan future, "social value groups" in the society of tomorrow. Experience and materialist ideology alike had taught these children to look for a self-interested motive behind every human act. A person who was kind to them must, therefore, be either a homosexual with designs on their bodies or a Nazi spy wanting to use them as informers. The idea that the human soul has a thousand shades of feeling, that at times all logical reasoning is submerged in the depth of the soul, the idea that someone might wish to stretch out a hand towards them simply because they were helpless and weak, would have been completely unacceptable and confusing to these children, and would have roused profound suspicion. So I became a "commissar" in their eyes; they believed that I was "organizing" them on the express instructions of the Buchenwald Communists. The perverse wickedness of the Nazi machinery had managed to paralyze their youthful souls, transforming them into cold little human machines. The ten-year-olds could still cry, but not the fourteen-year-olds, who were impudent, bullying and dangerous.

On that night when I first caught sight of those three little shivering sparrows, I had no world-shaking plans for these children. Nothing could have been further from my mind than to become for them a symbol of Western democracy, the capitalist system, and faith in God and fatherland. But, without my willing it, that in time became my role. It sometimes happens in life that one is caught up in the mighty flood of circumstances and carried away by the tide. Those whom the waves carry farther than the others become the leaders, whether they like it or not. That is what happened to me in Berga-Elster.

I wish to state here that I was acting neither as an agent of the decadent West, nor of the cartels, nor was I in the pay of the Secret Service. I could not have been a hireling of the Western democracies, because all I knew of them was only through hearsay. And I am willing to declare on oath that I had not been commissioned by the international plutocratic Bolsheviks to poison young souls on their behalf.

Next morning, at the *Appel*, sixteen children crowded around me. The *Lagerältester* – a German Communist – growled at me, saying that I should have lined the children up in a separate group. He, too, believed that I was the special agent of Buchenwald. Thus the seventeen of us stood in a separate group. Then in came the SS Hauptsturmführer, a man of middle age, with the infamous skull and cross-bones adorning his uniform cap. Without a word he passed by the two thousand men until he reached our little group. And then a miracle happened. A smile stole on to the face of the SS officer. He even smiled like a human being. He stroked the children's heads and turned to me.

"You must take good care of these children. Is that understood?"

"Yes, Herr Hauptsturmführer."

"Not a hair of their heads must be touched while I am here."

"Yes, sir."

"Take them to the kitchen to peel potatoes. You go with them and look after them."

"Yes, sir."

He turned to the *Lagerältester*. "I hold this young man responsible for seeing that no harm comes to them. Do you understand?"

"Yes, Herr Hauptsturmführer," the *Lagerältester* stammered, never having seen such a thing before.

Again the SS officer spoke to me. "Take care of them, Junge."

"Yes, sir, I shall take care of them."

And I marched the youngsters off towards the kitchen.

The eyes were popping out of the head of Hans Kapo, the prisoner in charge of the kitchen, as we entered in a body. Then he swore:

"I wanted spud-peelers – and they send me teat-suckers!"

He looked each child up and down as if he were a repulsive monstrosity, his face contorted into a frightening grimace, so that the youngsters huddled together in horror.

But Schlosser, the Vorarbeiter (foreman), assessed our invasion from a different angle. He turned to me, and from behind his huge, black-rimmed spectacles subjected me to a microscopic survey.

"And who are you?" asked Schlosser. "What do you want here?"

This man Schlosser was a rare specimen as far as ugly men go. He looked like a half-formed, decadent gorilla. In the most unusual places – for instance, in the centre of his forehead – his bristly hair curled forth from under his skin. In place of a moustache black threads dangled downward from his nostrils, and dark rivulets of hair gushed from his ears. Schlosser was hunchbacked as well. Later we gave him the nickname of Quasimodo. Whether he was really deaf or merely impeded in his hearing by the hair protruding from his ears, we never managed to discover. But it remained a fact that Quasimodo not only asked everything twice, but expected to be answered twice, too.

"What do you want here? What do you want here?"

"I am responsible for the children."

"What? WHAT?"

"I am responsible for the children."

"Who told you to come? Who told you to come?"

"The Hauptsturmführer, the Hauptsturmführer."

In the meantime Hans Kapo, engrossed in his own thoughts, was charging up and down between the two big stoves on which the concoction flatteringly known as vegetable stew was brewing.

While Schlosser was small and pot-bellied, Hans Kapo was tall and desiccated, at least six feet in height. The two of them seemed to me like a comedy couple, such as the Laurel and Hardy team in old films. As Kapo was racing up and down, I noticed that he placed his feet somewhat apart after the fashion of sailors. Undoubtedly, Hans Kapo must have been a sailor once.

Suddenly he stopped.

"Well, a Social Democrat has certain feelings," he shouted at the children. "A Social Democrat can't throw these unfortunate bastards out into the gutter. All right. Sit down, and get cracking with the peeling."

Both these men spoke in *"Hochdeutsch"* (High German); both wore the red triangle with the Capital D in the middle which showed that they were Reichsdeutsche, Imperial German citizens.

Schlosser, who was jealous of me over my position, turned to Kapo and said: "And what about him, what about him?"

The Social Democrat turned towards me.

"Are you a Jew?"

"Yes." Frightened, Schlosser repeated: *"Jude, Jude"* (Jew, Jew).

"Well, as far as I'm concerned," continued the Social Democrat, bellowing, "I will not work with Jews. I'd rather resign."

There was silence. Schlosser nodded his head so violently that he must have felt quite dizzy.

"That pig," Kapo went on, "that National Socialist SS of a pig, obviously didn't know that this hook-nosed bastard is a Jew."

Another short pause ensued.

A bald, round-faced Pole emerged from the other end of the kitchen. He was nibbling away at a boiled potato which must have been too hot, judging by the way he threw it from one hand to the other to cool it.

"Which one is the Jew?" he asked innocently.

Hans Kapo bawled at him: "Have you no eyes in your head, you idiotic bastard? That one with the big, crooked konk, that's the Jew."

I was beginning to be fed up with this Jew-controversy when, as Kapo was advancing threateningly with the intention of kicking me out of the kitchen, Ivan the Russian boy intervened. Ivan could have made little sense of the shouting, but he must have realized that I was going to be kicked out. So he yelled something, in

Russian, at the Pole. There was a brief silence; then the Pole turned to Hans Kapo.

"If you don't want to burn your fingers, you'd better leave the Jew alone."

"Why?" Kapo demanded noisily.

"Yes, why? Why?" Schlosser inquired.

"Buchenwald has put him in charge of the children," the Pole said softly and bit into the potato.

"Buchenwald has put him in charge of the children" – it sounded as though he had said: "Auntie Mary has put him in charge of the children. If you make a nuisance of yourself, you'll find yourself up against Auntie Mary."

Kapo swallowed hard. "Since when do they put Jews in charge at Buchenwald?"

There was no answer. Kapo paced up and down. After five minutes he pulled up in front of me.

"You aren't a Jew. Right?"

"I am a Jew."

"You can't be a Jew!"

By now I had had enough.

"Listen, Kapo," I said, I am a Jew whether you like it or not. Furthermore, whether you like it or not, I am going to stay here with the children. Furthermore, you're going to get a bigger kick in your arse from me, and from the kids, and from Buchenwald than you've ever had in your life – unless you shut that filthy big mouth of yours."

With protruding eyes he stared at me.

I went on: "Well now. I am responsible for what happens to these children. So it will be better for you if you keep that refined Social Democratic mouth of yours shut. And if I catch you uttering the word 'Jew' just once more, then I promise, Hans Kapo, you won't live to see the no-so-distant end of the war."

For the first time, he glanced at me as if I were a human being. Then he scratched his head.

"You haven't got a sense of humor?" he said. "I was only joking."

"I was joking, too," I said with a straight face.

After that, we started peeling the potatoes.

# CHAPTER XVI

It was a cold, cruel winter. Outside, our fellow prisoners, who were being used by the Germans for building a factory in the depths of the mountains, were dying like flies, day after day. But the youngsters and I did not suffer either from cold or from hunger in the kitchen. The huge pots were warm, and if we felt hungry there was always some boiled potato to be had. In fact, after a time we all put on weight there.

By now the young people had come to realize that their protector was not the agent of Buchenwald, nor was he a homosexual or a Communist. The hours we spent together among the ovens had drawn us all nearer to one another. Their young minds, thirsty for knowledge, looked to me for answers to the many questions which, during the nightmarish course of the past years, they had not even learned to formulate. We talked about God, about democracy, about the world we hoped for after the war – a world where one would have enough to eat and be able to roam the streets freely, where everybody would be able to think what he liked and say what he thought. In the long nights we spoke at times about the worlds beyond the world, about the stars whose light must travel thousands upon thousands of years before reaching our earth. We wondered if there was life on the planets that we saw sparkling in the frozen night through the kitchen windows. They continually asked me if there had ever been in the history of mankind a time such as this, whether there had ever lived other Hitlers who had destroyed other people by fiery furnaces. They inquired about the differences between Judaism and Christianity, and whether Jesus was really the Son of God. Their instructors in Buchenwald had not discussed any of these questions with them. These were the voices of freedom speaking in the kitchen, during our day- or night-shift duties. Often we were silent. Then, Ivan, accompanied by Boris, the night-duty cook, would sing Russian songs which cast over us the spell of the endless Russian steppes. We sang in Czech, too, and in German and Hungarian.

I would often pray to God. I thanked Him for my good fortune in having weathered the past months, and that now, fortified in body and soul, I had charge of sixteen young lives for whom I felt responsible. I felt these days that, in my own small way, I was part of creation: and I sensed within myself something of that vast Power that was responsible for me. I felt that God frequently works out His plans through human beings, and that if only we listen to human words and voices, we can often hear Him speak. And whenever I succeeded in bringing curiosity, interest, a smile, or sometimes tears into the eyes of these wretched children and felt proud of myself for it, I also thought that in my very self-praise I was praising that Infinite power who had granted me the opportunity of playing a positive role in this inferno. I felt that I had strength only because He was present in my blood and in my senses, and that so long as I realized this Force within me, the Germans would be unable to touch me.

Then spring came. The days grew longer, the air warmer. The earth drank in the snow and the mountains of Berga-Elster surrounded us with a wreath of green. And with the spring-time, desire began to live again within me. Sometimes I woke up knowing that I had been weeping in my sleep, without knowing why. In my dreams I was often with Eva, and at the very moment of our union I would awake into the dreary present, my heart pounding wildly.

And suddenly, one night, the miracle happened – the miracle for which the oppressed peoples of the world had been waiting.

We were on night duty. The huge pots hissed on the stove; the boys were peeling the potatoes in silence. Outside a wild storm was raging, and every now and then the lights would turn dim. With my eyes closed I sat leaning back against the warmth of one of the ovens, filled with a sense of wellbeing that I had not experienced for a long time. Ivan was singing, and his voice seemed to reach my ears from thousands of miles away. Suddenly I felt as if the ground had been jerked from under my feet.

Ivan's song came to an abrupt end. I opened my eyes. There was a silence, and then Boris whispered: "The earth is shaking."

"They're bombing," said David, the Polish-Jewish boy.

Boris shook his head. "That is the voice of freedom ... they're big guns."

We ran out into the open and strained our ears in the night. From beyond the mountains a slow, muffled thudding could be heard. But now and again a gust of wind brought the sound of the guns more clearly.

Boris was crying. Tears came to my eyes, too.

"Is it true? Can it be true?"

But in the depth of my heart I knew that these sounds were indeed the first voices of freedom.

We went back into the kitchen. Boris leaned his head on his hand and wept. Ivan said:

"We were standing in our garden when the Germans appeared. They leveled their guns at us. Then my father stepped in front of my mother, and there was a bang, and he fell slowly to the ground. It was just like a big oak tree being felled. And now the guns are roaring...."

The sound of the guns reverberated through all the nights that followed.

One evening grey, melancholy clouds drew a veil over the spring sky, bringing with them a lowering of the spirit. I had just come off duty and was in the bare factory building in which we slept when someone addressed me.

"Mr. Heimler, my dear young gentleman," a pale man, as thin as skeleton, was saying to me. "You do remember me surely. I am Joska, sir. Joska Nyari, the gipsy, from the café on the corner. Don't you recognize me, young gentleman?"

No, I did not remember him. I looked for the old, familiar features in the lines of his face, but I could discover no one I knew in that distorted mask.

"I've not got long to live, young sir."

Only then did I notice that the man was sick, and very sick at that. I saw that he could hardly move on his bunk and that the words issued with difficulty from his lips. It did not matter whether I knew him personally or not. This man was a compatriot. He knew the town in which I had once lived, he belonged to my past.

"Don't you remember, young sir, I used to court Mariska who worked at your house? But she wouldn't have anything to do with me, she wouldn't." A heavy groan accompanied his words.

"When did they bring you here, Joska?"

"When? Not so very long ago. Just a few months. After the Jews, they rounded up the gypsies. I don't even know what happened to the wife and children. The younger kid can play the fiddle already, that he can! And I'm going to kick the bucket here. They won't even know where I was buried. Tell me, young sir, does one get buried here at all?"

"I don't know, Joska, but don't you worry your head about death."

My heart filled with memories. Joska I could not recall, but I did remember the gipsy music of the corner café, sobbing every night among the chestnut trees. I recalled the nights long ago when, as a small child, I lay in my cot while Father and Mother went down to the café for a black coffee. I remembered the rattle of the quaint little tram-cars which broke into the gipsy music every few minutes. Oh, yes, and I did remember Maris also. How could I have failed to remember her, when for eight long years she had lived with us as a member of the family? In this grim factory building through which the draught was howling I could hear within my head the noises of old summer nights. Laughter from the street, the echo of feet, squeals, now and again a deeper voice – their pattern remained within my ear. Who knew what had become of the people who paraded along the Corso to the music of the gipsy band? Who knew where, into what corner of the world, the war had cast the people who had listened to Joska Nyari's music? Joska Nyari, Joska, Joska....

Tears welled up in my eyes. What could I do for this man? What could I do to stop him from perishing so miserably?

For a long time Joska was silent, then he said:

"Young sir, I've done a lot of wrong in my day, I've done many wicked things. I feel I won't live till the morning. I would like to confess."

"There is no priest here, Joska, my friend."

"Isn't there?" he asked, staring ahead of him rigidly. "Well, then, perhaps the Lord God won't mind if I confess to you. Please hear my confession."

"Well, Joska, go on, make your confession."

I could see from the contorted features of his face that a great struggle was taking place in his soul.

"What's a sin, young gentleman?" he asked with imploring eyes. "That I went with women? That I got married twice in front of the priest, even while my first wife was still alive? Is that a sin? Tell me to my face, is it a sin?"

"If you feel it to be a sin, Joska, then it is a sin."

"I feel it is," he said sobbing. "Twice I stood before the altar, because the second one had money, three thousand pengos. They'll roast me in hell, won't they?" Then, as though speaking to himself, he said:

"Makes no difference now if they do burn me, it won't be any worse than rotting away here. It won't be any worse, will it?

"Well, that's my chief sin. I confess it, it's the honest truth. It was the first wife I loved. Even now I love her. Will you do something for me, young gentleman?"

"What is it you want, Joska?"

"If ever the Lord Jesus should lead you back home, go to the gipsy settlement, you know where it is, behind Vizmellek Street. Look up Mrs. Nyari, the real one, and tell her that I was a wicked man, and ask her to forgive me. Tell her that. You won't be ashamed to go to the gipsy settlement, will you? Well, tell me … tell me you will."

"When I get home, Joska, I promise I shall go."

"And if they're hard up, go and see Kantor, the inn-keeper. I left my fiddle with him; sell it, my young sir. If you sell it, young gentleman, you can make a better bargain of it; they'd cheat them right and left."

"All right, set your mind at rest. I shall see to everything."

"And I never stole, young sir. Do believe me, I didn't steal. Once the police sergeant came to see me and said

177

that I had stolen some gent's silk scarf from the cloakroom. He wanted to have me locked up. Well, I never stole it. Do tell the wife, Mrs. Nyari, that I never stole in my life. That is all, young sir! And now I am very tired. I want to sleep. May the good Lord bless you."

I stepped out into the cool spring evening. The clouds had withdrawn from the sky, and above the mountains the stars sparkled with crystal radiance. I wanted to help. But how? What is justice? What is the Power that forgives? In what way had I any more right to live than Joska Nyari? Perhaps there were some people in the camp who, if only they could survive, could give something to the world. But from where could one expect help? The end of the war was at hand. Perhaps it would be only a matter of weeks, of days – and yet men were doomed to perish before even beholding the faces of their liberators.

I set out towards the hospital barrack. I ought to get Joska Nyari into hospital. Yes, I'll speak to one of the doctors. They'll listen to me. I am supposed to have some authority here.

Who merits life and who death? What can one regard as a standard? Greatness … what sort of greatness? I entered the ward. Without a word, the prisoner standing at the door allowed me to pass. He knew me from the kitchen. I found a fellow countryman of mine and begged him to get Joska Nyari admitted into the hospital. He came with me to the barrack. Bending down over Joska, he unbuttoned the filthy shirt on his breast and listened for a few minutes in silence. Then he stood up and said:

"This man is dead." And when he saw how deeply this news touched me, he shrugged his shoulders. "Such things happen in life."

Ever since the noise of the guns had first been heard in the distance, a great uneasiness had possessed the camp. Wherever I went I heard excited discussions. When the men came back after work, they told at the evening roll call how the atmosphere had changed even at work. The German civilian workers were beginning to be friendlier. They would chat with the prisoners; they no longer swore at them as they used to do before. The American prisoners of war, who were working on the banks of the Elster, were in a better mood, too, and if a prisoner from our camp passed by they would wink at him gaily. Even those at the end of their tether found fresh strength since the guns had been heard.

I witnessed some strange scenes during these days. People expected a miracle to happen. In the sick ward some of the doctors held spiritualist séances, hoping to find out what the future had in store. Physicians solidly grounded in scientific medicine, who only the day before would have ridiculed any such foolishness, sat there among the flickering candles awaiting, pale-faced, the response of the spirits. But this queer uneasiness obsessed not only them, but the masses also. One night a star shone brighter than usual. The prisoners pointed at the sky.

"It is written in the holy books that at the end of the massacre the Lord will kindle the star of peace in heaven," they murmured.

The sound of the guns grew louder than ever. Then one morning the SS command ordered a special roll call. This *Appel* was unusually long. Suddenly a wave of restlessness broke out among the lines, and the prisoners broke rank – an unprecedented act. However much the camp police swore and yelled, they could not restore order. The crowds swayed to and fro as if all of a sudden they had caught some unknown fever. At that moment the SS officer, Schwarzbach, appeared, with the camp commandant Hauptsturmführer Schimmel. Some of the prisoners were singing the Marseillaise, others the International; others were just shouting wildly, meaninglessly. At last the SS officer fired into the air, and order was restored. Then Schimmel spoke:

"Jews, Communists, rascals! You can hear the American guns, can't you? But don't you worry. You won't hear them for long."

He went on to say that we were to march eastward. The camp would be evacuated. Anyone who could not keep up with the others would be shot dead – also those who attempted to escape. Yet his words left us with no sense of alarm after the *Appel* was over.

At about noon we heard the news that the Americans had occupied Buchenwald.

Next morning, in long columns, we marched out of the camp. The children were walking just behind me. For the last time I glances back at Berga-Elster: on the electric clock at the station time still stood at half past twelve.

# CHAPTER XVII

Day and night the SS marched us farther away from the ever-increasing thunder of the guns. Their plan, according to rumor, was to reach the camp of Mauthausen. Schwarzbach, the commander, was driving us through the vast forest known as the Schwarzenberg – a black brook leading us over a black mountain. The majority of the SS men escorting us hailed from the Schwaibian settlements in Western Hungary. Their fear of the morrow was written in their faces. These Schwabians were men of evil appearance. They were not merely traitors to their country of adoption, but also murderers. Still, now that the guns were sounding loud behind us and they felt the iron grip of the Allies tightening around their throats, they would now and again slip us a chunk of bread. Not out of kindness, certainly not prompted by human fellow feeling, but only because of their own fear and cowardice. Anyone who fell was shot dead at Schwarzbach's command, and the road behind us was strewn with corpses.

It was a cold spring evening, at the end of the tenth day of our march. There were a few clouds in the sky, and as we sat by the roadside in the forest I gazed up at the trees and the sky, and as I used to do when I was a child I tried to form pictures from the ever-changing shape of the clouds. For a few minutes it was a map of Hungary, then the face of a Roman soldier, then Moses, then a woman in love opening her arms – and then the wind dispersed the clouds, destroying all my pictures.

For three days we had been without food. Now hunger and the enforced march were having a strange effect on my senses. I felt for a moment as if I had stepped out of my body and had become a part of the world outside myself. I was part of the trees as they swayed in the breeze, part of the sky above and the changing shapes of the clouds, part of the stony ground beneath my feet. I felt that there was no such thing as life and no such thing as death, only that there was something eternal beyond the blue and beyond my beating heart. And this concept of eternity made me realize just how vain all the objects are for which man strives. And I stepped out of time, and years and hours and minutes became in my mind something created by man and of no importance. Then, like a wild beast, hunger began to gnaw at my inside, and the hunger of the soul was followed by the hunger of the flesh. Dark shadows appeared before my eyes, and the jungle within me reverberated to the sound of the wild beast crying "eat and kill – and eat again." And still they gave us no food.

Night fell and the stars shone down between the gathering clouds, and at last food arrived. It was boiled rice. As we queued up I noticed that the beast in the jungle was raving not only within me but within others also, as, like animals thirsting for blood, we poor pariahs waited for our masters to dole out our food. In spite of the measures enforced by the SS, it was impossible for them to maintain order as we smelled the food, sensed the source of life not eternal but physical.

It was then that I caught sight of an old man, on all fours, trying to find a place in the queue. Each time he tried to move in he was kicked to the side of the road, screaming aloud with pain. Suddenly this man became tremendously important to me, and I would have been willing to sacrifice my place, my food, my own life, to help him on to his feet, to drag him into the queue so that he could eat. He was much too weak to stand on his feet, but I fought the crowd, I fought the pack of wild beasts, kicking and biting and scratching until they moved aside and opened up a gap; and as I took my place the old man was behind me, dragging himself along the ground. When the food was given out and my turn came I gave the first plate to him, and not until I had watched him licking it clean as he sat by the roadside did I eat my own food. Then I felt that whatever wrongs I had committed previously in my life, the slate was now clean.

One night the blond young murderer Schwarzbach ordered his men to shoot the lot of us. Scared of what might happen, the rest of the SS thugs refused to obey his orders. So, on a charge of stealing bread, the commander himself butchered several of our fellow prisoners in the sight of all of us. Then, with the satisfaction of one who had done a good job well, he mounted his motorcycle and rode off, and we never saw him again.

After the flight of their commander, the SS men tore the badge of skull and crossbones from their collars. Some of them even went so far as to offer us cigarettes. Eventually we arrived at the outskirts of a small German town. That was a strange night. Beneath us lay the town, behind us the immense forest – and beyond the forest, down in the valley, the flash of the firing guns was visible. We were quartered in a stable, and we awaited dawn in sleepless excitement, for the thunder of the bombardment kindled a hope within us that the Americans might occupy the town during the same night. But when the sun rose we were still prisoners, and by morning the gunfire had ceased. In the streets women were walking to the market, their baskets on their arms; freshly washed linen hung on the clothes lines. Now the silence was terrifying. From the manor house next to our stable yard a German woman offered water to the prisoners. This was the first time in Germany that I had experienced any willingness to help on the part of the population. Up to now, fists had been raised against us on all sides; wherever we had gone, the children had stoned us, and the adults had shouted to the SS: "Why don't you shoot those scoundrels dead?" – to receive the smiling assurance: "Better late than never."

Now the SS no longer bothered to guard the camp. Many of the prisoners had escaped, others just roamed aimlessly about the town. The behavior of the population towards us was as yet undecided: they could not make up their minds definitely what attitude to adopt. They loathed us, and at the same time were afraid of us. If they did help it was because they were scared of the future, and because both our physical appearance and what we told them about the camps aroused their apprehension that vengeance would be devastating and horrible. Boys of twelve and fourteen who the day before had marched in these very streets with machine-guns in their hands, now hid their weapons and their uniforms and once again put on short trousers. But however much they tried to look like children, most of them were in fact murderers. It was from among them that the *Volkssturm* had been recruited – a fanatical organization established for the express purpose of hunting us down. Now they had been warned by their commanders that the democratic powers would not harm unarmed "children."

My own group of youngsters called a meeting in one corner of the stable. Ten of them had decided to flee to the forest and await the Americans there. In the course of the discussion two more boys joined them so that only four of us were left who opposed this risky undertaking. I told them that we ought to wait until we had crossed the Czech frontier. Among a friendly population it should be easier to escape than in Germany, where the inhabitants might turn against us suddenly if circumstances permitted.

The behavior of the SS during the past days had changed to such an extent that it was highly improbable, now that their leaders had fled and they themselves were afraid for their lives, that they would resort to further atrocities. I said that we ought to continue marching with them towards the east; that this was the wrong time to escape. But the twelve children felt that every moment spent in proximity to the SS was dangerous, and that one could never know what these murderers might decide to do at the last moment. I did not try to force my opinion upon them, for I should not have like to shoulder the responsibility for it if I had been wrong, so we said farewell to one another and they disappeared into the dark in the course of that same night.

In the morning the SS marched us on, towards the east.

One afternoon, after a merciless forced march that went on for several days, we reached the Czech frontier. The village at which we had arrived was Manetin; a huge advertisement of Bata shoes loomed large on its outskirts. Here, by order of the SS, we were to rest. It was now the end of April: the soil was warm and the meadows bright with flowers. Farther down the road the wind whirled the dust high into the air; above us the clouds embraced. The setting sun shone on the unshaven faces of my comrades, worn beyond recognition. As a result of the escapes and the murders, what had once been a regiment of two thousand prisoners had now dwindled to a bare four hundred. I stood up and looked around. I wanted to engrave on my memory every detail of this sad sight, so that later, across the gulf of time, I might remember it thus, a dramatic bas-relief in my mind. For I knew that we had reached the end of our journey and of our servitude. I stood and gazed at the crowd of pitiful men, their disfiguring sores apparent through their prison uniforms. I looked at them as they stared, with glazed eyes, into nothingness, or into the sky which, behind the racing clouds, flaunted the color of its own freedom and infinity. Somewhere in the middle of the large group an old man lay on his back, grasping at his heart, with the sweat running down his face. All of a sudden I remembered my father – he, too, used often to complain of his heart. I walked over to this unknown man. He was French, and I could not understand the words that fell, hardly audible, from his lips. He seemed to be asking for something, but no one near us knew any French. Kneeling beside him I asked him in German what he wanted, but he did not understand me. Then suddenly a Latin word became audible: "*Aqua, aqua.*" There was no water anywhere. The SS men were standing huddled in a small group, discussing something excitedly. I had never before asked anything of those murderers: in the concentration camp to address an SS man was equivalent to instant death. But now I was not afraid. I imagined that it was my own father who was lying there – and if not my father, then somebody else's father, somebody else's husband. The thought crossed my mind that at that very moment some French boy might be leaning over my father, as he whispered "*Aqua, aqua.*"

The group of the SS stared at me in amazement when I asked them for water. I had spoken to them in Hungarian, since all of them were Schwabian settlers from Hungary. One of them reached for his flask and gave it to me without word. I took it to the old Frenchman and let him drink. Then I washed his forehead, wiped off the perspiration and dried him with my shirtsleeve. His large blue eyes opened wide at me, and again he seemed to resemble my father. Gratefully he whispered: "*Merci, merci.*"

When I sat down again, by myself, a great peace enveloped me. "Perhaps there is still hope that I will see my father again. Maybe the Germans have not killed him after all. Perhaps we shall be able to build up a new life together over the ruins." And then, suddenly, without any particular reason, it began to grieve me that I had so often hurt my beloved "old man." During the war years, how often had he been annoyed with me when, despite the laws for the protection of racial purity (which meant imprisonment for any offender), I had chased after *"shiksahs"* (Christian girls) – and even got one of them into trouble; or when in the middle of the war, I had arrived home at three in the morning after a drinking bout with my friends, as he had been on the point of getting the police to search for me. Yes, I had been a fine good-for-nothing; I had hurt my dear father many a time. As I grew into an adolescent, how often had I behaved rudely towards him, accusing him of living in a dream, of "neglecting his family for the sake of his principles." How those words used to pain him! "O Father, if only I could see you once more! There is nothing in heaven or earth I would not do for you. I will make a home for your sick and weary body. Never again will I raise my voice against you. Father, my father, come back to me. It is to you and to Mother that I owe everything in life. Father, do not forsake me!"

Tears flooded my eyes. It had been very difficult to make contact with my father after my childhood was over. When I became an adolescent an invisible wall had risen between us, and all the understanding and love which I felt towards him somehow came to be held back behind this barrier. In times of trouble I always fled to my mother; it was she who had been my friend and companion. Father had loomed over me like a large and menacing shadow. "You were too big for me, Father; far

too big for me to bear." But now, on the outskirts of
Manetin, this wall came tumbling down, and through my
tears I was looking towards the east, towards my country,
towards the future, and I trembled as I thought of the
possible fate of my father, a great man broken by
adversity.

We started off again, and as soon as we reached the
first houses we saw that we had arrived home. From the
windows women and men with tear-stained eyes watched
our melancholy march-past; girls ran up to us to hand us a
lump of bread, or some article of clothing. In the centre of
the village the crowd was lining the pavement like a guard
of honor, waving their handkerchiefs at us as though we
were returning victorious from the war.

And then a young girl ran out of the crowd and threw
her arms around the neck of one of my wretched filthy
companions. Weeping, these strangers kissed each other,
like father and daughter or as long-lost brother and sister.
At once the whole line broke up, and the women, young
and old alike, covered us with their kisses. And through
us they kissed their own loved ones whom the war had
carried away. Shaken and moved, we clung to these
unknown women, hugging through their warm bodies the
life which seemed to have been running out of us so
fearfully fast.

The SS led us to an evacuated school building; and
here the women brought large pots of soup, and we were
able to look into their tearful faces with our bellies full for
the first time since the beginning of our wandering. Then
came the Czech gendarmes, who embraced us and spoke
to us with as much love as if they had been our brothers.
But slowly the mood changed. Bitterly the women turned
towards our SS guards, shaking their clenched fists in the
air: "Murderers, you'll pay for this!" The men of the
village paraded threateningly around the school. Our

guards were terrified, and after a brief discussion decided to take us back to German territory. And then we four youngsters, who had stayed together since the rest of our band escaped, came to a momentous decision. Quoting the words of our great poet: "This is the time; now or never," we went to the latrine, clambered over the fence, and within a few minutes were swallowed up in the forest.

We were free – at last.

# CHAPTER XVIII

It was only a few days since we had set out from Manetin on our homeward way.

The German armies were still holding out, the war was still on, yet on the roofs of the Czech houses the national flag fluttered in the wind. Cistaj – that was the name of the small Czech village in which we first beheld the tired, dusty features of our liberators. Then we heard the last broadcast from the Fuehrer's General Headquarters.

On May 8, a sun-drenched day, we heard with pounding hearts that we had won.

We had won. Won what? The war? Yes. Freedom? Yes. But at what price? I wanted to be alone, to think for a while. This news was almost too much to bear. I had to sort out in my mind what this victory meant and how much it meant to me.

Behind the farm-house where we were staying was a large field and beyond this were some trees. Above them rose a blue and majestic sky. The silence was absolute: the only sound to be heard was the dull thud of my feet on the earth as I walked across the field. Suddenly I became aware that the silence was within me, too – a silence such as there must have been before the days of creation, before the heavens and the stars and the chaotic, yet law-abiding world were formed. This was the silence of eternal peace, the continuous silence of eternal time. But the world had taken shape, the great forces had been set in motion – the sun with loving compulsion to maintain the earth and a myriad of stars to spin in space – and man had been created in the image of God. And man heard his

190

voice for the first time, and in his own voice he recognized the voice of the Infinite, and he gazed up at the great blue above and began to weep. And because of the force of gravity his tears fell downwards to the earth, but because of the force of God his soul soared upwards to the heavens. And this, I felt in that moment, would always be the destiny of man.

Then I began to cry. I fell down on to the deep brown earth and breathed in the smell of the fields, and it was good. And the silence was broken by the whisper of the wind, by the song of the birds and by the distant mooing of the cows in far-off meadows. Somewhere a dog was barking. And it was good.

I was part of the world and of the present again, and my tears had meaning because I had lost everything except my life. I knew that all the people I loved were dead. I knew that the freedom I had gained would be difficult to bear, and that it would be long before I found peace once more. I realized that I should go on searching for love.

At last I opened my eyes and rolled over on to my back, and as I did so I saw a girl approaching. Through my tears I could see that she was young and that she was frightened. She said something in Czech which I could not understand, and when I indicated this with a movement of my hands, she asked in broken German what I was doing there. I answered that I did not know. She came nearer, and when she saw my tears she was no longer frightened. Then she saw the triangle of the political prisoner with the prison number on my jacket – and she understood. She knelt down beside me in the field, and slowly, without either of us uttering word, tears gathered in her eyes, and soon our tears were intermingled on the earth. Then she spoke again in broken German: "I love you." "I love you too," I said. We gazed at each other, two young people unable to speak, but our hearts crying out to each other in a language louder than words. Then we kissed – and it was the first kiss of love I had received or given since Eva had died. There was no desire of flesh in this kiss, only desire of the soul, a pure desire for unity between man and woman. It was the kiss of a long-lost sister, a re-discovered mother, a wife who over the years has become part of oneself.

She went as she had come, but suddenly she stopped. "What is you name?" When I told her she repeated it: "Jancsi, Jancsi." Then she said "Yarnicsku" in Czech and slipped away and I never saw her again.

But I returned from that field like a newly awakened man who has just seen the world and knows that he is part of it and belongs to it. I felt that the funeral of my dear ones had begun, and I recognized the birth of my freedom.

When I returned to the house I heard the radio announcing that although the war was finished German guns were still firing on the beautiful buildings of ancient Prague. The Czechs begged us to stay on, but it was not possible – we wanted to go home. And at last, after a lengthy and difficult journey on foot, on the bumpers of trains, on the tops of trucks, we reached the Hungarian frontier.

I was lying in the garden, amid the flowers of summer, in the lush, caressing grass. For several days I had been coming here every afternoon to gaze at the window of the veranda where, once upon a time, Mother had hung out the washing. In the evening she used to come to this window, calling out, "Come, my son, supper is ready." Now behind the glass panes of the veranda strangers were living, strangers were hanging out their washing on the line – yet still I waited to see my Mother's face appear in the brown window-frame.

Weeds had overrun the garden; it had been neglected for years. The summer-house stood bare. Only the chestnut trees, swaying in the wind, were as of old. It was here that I had learnt to walk, here that I had fallen down for the first time. Here, in this garden, I searched for the past. Each pebble had a meaning, every leaf on the shrubs belonged to me, to my past, to the life of my family which had been scattered by the storm.

Beyond the gate, the town. My God, how it had changed; even the color of the houses was different. The town had died just as the people had died – and those who remained were dragging themselves through life, confused by the sense of guilt which they carried in their souls. From this once populous little town they had carried away six thousand human beings, of whom only a score had returned.

Not only this town, but my whole country seemed to have died. As I made my way homeward, everywhere I had seen burnt villages, devastated cities, unfriendly and disillusioned people. A short time before, the propaganda of ultimate victory was still being loudly declaimed: now everyone walked stealthily, not knowing when the hand of retribution would reach him.

As I lay there in the garden, all this seemed only a bad dream. "Up there on the veranda ... soon it will be evening and I shall go up and have supper with my family ..." But I could not go on playing this game for long: at any moment the concierge might come out of his basement flat – a new man, who knew nothing of the former days.

Yes, it was time for me to wake up to the truth, to life, to reality. I must face the unbelievable fact that my family was no longer alive. A holocaust had obliterated us, our town, the whole country. Of all my people I alone had come back from the jaws of death.

"And now, what will happen to me? I have nobody. I have come back from the hell of hells – why should I collapse now? Or shall I kill myself...?"

No. There were others whom I had to see, messages I had to deliver to the living from the dead. There were things I had to do, words I had to speak, moments which I had to dissect in order to show the world what I had seen and lived through, on behalf of the millions who had seen it also – but could not longer speak. Of their dead, burnt, bodies I would be the voice.

I threaded my way along the bank of a small stream towards the flat in which I had rented a room. "I must find new clothes in place of these torn rags. I must work – I am hungry – I'll have to eat. I must start everything from scratch. I must make something of my freedom...." And I began to walk back through the dead streets, back towards life.

# THE END

# About the Author

Eugene Heimler was born on March 27, 1922 in Szombathely, Hungary the son of a lawyer and prominent member of the social-democratic party. He became a successful poet in Hungary with two volumes of poetry published before he was twenty. At age 21 he was deported to Auschwitz and Buchenwald and survived with the help of his happy memories about his childhood and his beloved mother, who had died after a long illness shortly before the start of World War II.

His wife Eva, his father, sister and her little son were murdered in Auschwitz. In 1946 he married Lily, née Salgo and in 1947 Eugene and Lily immigrated to England. At Lily's untimely death (1984) she left two children, Susan and George.

Soon after he received his diploma as the first psychiatric social worker from Manchester University, he began to develop his own social-integrative method, which became well known in Europe, America and Canada under the name of *The Heimler Method of Social Functioning*.

Later on he returned to Germany in order to teach young Germans his unique approach in which frustration and suffering are used as potential for satisfaction and creativity, and as the means to find purpose and meaning in life. He became director of the *Hounslow Project on Community Care* (1965–71), consultant for the *Ministry of Social Security* in England, the *World Health Organization* and the *Government of the United States of America*.

For 20 years he taught his subject at the University of London, England and his fame lead to chairs at several universities in the USA and Canada.

In 1985 Eugene Heimler received an honorary doctorate from the University of Calgary, Canada, where he had taught his subject for 17 years.

On the day marking the 40th anniversary of the end of the war in Europe, he married Miriam Bracha with whom he spent the last, very happy and fulfilled years of his life. Dr. Heimler died on December 4th, 1990.

His work is being continued by practitioners, lecturers and researchers around the world.

**The Healing Echo**

by Eugene Heimler

After surviving the worst trauma in human history Eugene Heimler transformed his pain and suffering into a model of healing that illuminates secrets to learning how to thrive and overcome whatever obstacles are in your path.

In *The Healing Echo* Dr. Heimler teaches you his unique empowering self-help method – how to transform your frustration and destructive impulses into creativity and new opportunities for flourishing.

In his innovative approach he gives you tools to develop a more resilient way of dealing with the stresses in your life, to overcome problems and to find meaning and purpose.

In this book you can learn to help yourself by listening to your inner voice and thus hear your *healing echo*.

In this second powerfully written volume of Eugene Heimler's incredible life's journey from a persecuted Jewish child in a small town in Hungary to world-renowned writer, therapist and teacher, Heimler is on his way home to Hungary from the concentration camps of Germany, where he had lost all his family. On this journey he experiences many life-threatening moments: being on a train with a former German SS man; witnessing the brutal rape of his traveling companion by Russian thugs; attempts on his life and being arrested and charged with treason in Hungary.

Eventually he reaches England and remarries, but his trials are manifold. After hearing that the Secret Police are torturing his friends in Budapest, he realizes he can never return to Hungary and has a breakdown. When psychoanalysis helps him come back to life and regain his hope for the future, he is ready to act on an early ambition to become a writer and psychologist. He starts to write Night of the Mist, which has become a world classic, and becomes a psychiatric social worker, eventually becoming the County Psychiatric Social Work Organizer for the Middlesex County Council. These challenges have their obstacles as well, and Heimler vividly describes his work as a psychiatric social worker, including his refusal to give up on others – and himself. His experiences eventually lead to the development of a new method of therapy, which is today known as the Heimler Method of Social Functioning.

Throughout his life, Heimler consistently fought to help victims gain the courage to become victors. In A Link in the Chain, also published as My Life After Auschwitz he once more tells his stories poetically and vividly.

*.....Messages.........*

A Survivor's Letter to a
Young German

**Eugene Heimler**

# MESSAGES
## *A Survivor's Letter to a Young German*

Eugene Heimler, in his captivatingly poetic style, takes you with him on a life-transforming journey through seas of imagination and rivers of tears; from storms of pain to pools of individual and communal wisdom as well as deep inside his self and yours.

His universal and autobiographical stories, like the vivid colors on the canvas of a water-color artist, flow and dynamically blend time dimensions into an expanding, cohesive whole.

The diversity of genre, time and metaphor is startling and reveals multiple layers of our physical, emotional and spiritual reality.

The author transcends time as he interweaves past, present and future into a tapestry of deep meaning and passion, stained by blood and marked by tears and joy.

This book is about the author's journey of losing, searching and re-finding his own identity and place in his physical, emotional and spiritual worlds.

In his "stream of consciousness" musings Heimler crosses time from biblical through medieval to modern human experiences of transformation through pain to self-discovery.

This artful intimate intertwining of personal, particular and universal themes draws the reader into Heimler's awe-inspiring multi-layered world of courageous introspection.

*Messages* illuminates how Heimler, as a Holocaust survivor, struggles to re-discover meaning, purpose and passion from his once shattered world.

Working through these challenges leads him to existential questions about the very meaning of life:

What are the connections between life and what we call death?

How can meaning transcend suffering?

How can we find peace if we deny our worst hours?

How can we understand all the hatred that surrounds us?

How can hate be turned into creativity instead of self-destructiveness?

What can keep our love and our ability to love alive in the midst of atrocities or indifference?

Come, join this remarkable man in his quest for eternal wisdom!

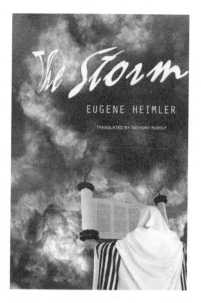

# THE STORM

THE STORM is a powerful drama in verse that reveals the secret of the survival of the Jewish people and how the Jews have been able to overcome history's never-ending challenges.

The drama is rooted in the author's personal Nazi death-camp experiences and his ongoing meditation on the Jewish tragedy of Masada. It illuminates how societal barbarism enabled Romans, Christians and Nazis to avoid and deny personal responsibility for their hatred, cruelty and massacres. Yet, despite a history punctuated by atrocities, Heimler breathes hope into the future for Jews, by voicing God's affirmation of the eternity of their survival.

This masterpiece is particularly relevant today, as extremism, antisemitism and intolerance sweep like wild fire across university campuses as well as Western- and Middle Eastern societies. The timeless message of Dr. Heimler's deeply moving drama is needed now more than ever before, to penetrate souls and educate minds.

What began as a teenager's innocent, promising verse grew, through the nightmare of the Shoah, into a profound, mature human soul, plumbing the depths of history, philosophy and faith.

*Rabbi Dr. André Ungar, New Jersey*


Eugene Heimler is a true Jewish hero of the twentieth century.

*Ronald A. Lewis, M.Ed.*

Can one benefit from suffering, pain and frustration? Prof. Dr. Eugene Heimler claims that, what we experience as frustration, is our potential for satisfaction. Based on his method of Social Functioning we can transform our weakness and what we call 'negative' into strength and to our own satisfaction as well as to the benefit of society. A certain amount of frustration serves as a driving force in our lives, that we need in order to be creative.

In this book, using case studies, Heimler describes how we can create a balance of satisfaction and frustration by means of the use of his method of Social Functioning and of the Heimler Scale, by observing and listening to ourselves.

Eugene Heimler's self-help-method of Social Functioning was developed and tested and proved extraordinarily successful.

In Constructive Use of Destructive Forces also published as Survival in Society Heimler describes in detail his interviewing and therapy techniques with individuals, couples and groups. His goal is to help them use their inner resources and past experiences.

The Heimler Method is applied with those needing therapy as well as 'healthy' individuals who want to explore their unused potential; it is used by teachers to help students become more creative; in the relationship between employers and employees; as well as by social workers and other helping professions.

## NAPFOGYATKOZÁS UTÁN

A Nyugat-magyarországi Szombathelyen született, boldog családban nőtt fel. Szülőhazájának kedves tája és kultúrája, valamint a zsidó szellemi örökségéhez való szenvedélyes kötődés vette körül. 17 éves korában jelent meg első verseskötete: az ártatlanság, a gyengédség és a csodálatos ígéret versei.

"...Mikor még gyerek voltam anyám azt akarta, hogy költő legyek. Egy téli estén az ölében ültem s megvallotta, hogy ez a titkos vágya..."

## *Daughter of Abraham*

For anyone on a life journey through pain towards transformation, Miriam Bracha Heimler's intimate, powerful memoir will help deepen your determination to overcome life's seemingly insurmountable obstacles.

Through touching vignettes Heimler paints vivid portraits of her continuing life challenges:

She escapes Communist East Germany as an 11 year old just before the rise of the Berlin Wall, leaving her Nazi father behind.

Despite her manifold struggles to overcome loneliness and poverty in her strange new world, and in defiance of having to fight peers' prejudice and feelings of inadequacy, she succeeds.

She makes many growth-steps on her way through the gates of her spiritual development.

Heimler's endearing, earthy, captivating style draws the reader into her multi-layered inner world of imagination, determination and hope.

The depth of the scenes she paints is reminiscent of great literature of the past, rather than superficial current works. The reader will enrich her / his life by diving into this real life treasure of vulnerability.

Made in the USA
Coppell, TX
01 November 2021